Teste deinen Englisch-Wortschatz

humboldt-Taschenbücher, Cassetten-Packages und CD-ROMs aus der Reihe Sprachen

Englisch	ISBN 3-581-
Englisch in 30 Tagen*	67051-8
Englisch für Fortgeschrittene*	66061-X
Englischer Basiswortschatz	66574-3
Englische Grammatik – kurz und schmerzlos	66617-0
Schluß mit typischen Englisch-Fehlern!	66664-2
Teste deinen Englisch-Wortschatz	66723-1

Französisch	
Französisch in 30 Tagen*	67052-6
Französisch für Fortgeschrittene	66109-8
Französischer Basiswortschatz	66696-0

Italienisch	
Italienisch in 30 Tagen*	67053-4
Italienisch für Fortgeschrittene	66108-X
Italienischer Basiswortschatz	66697-9

Spanisch	
Spanisch in 30 Tagen*	67054-2
Spanisch für Fortgeschrittene*	66626-X
Spanischer Basiswortschatz	66698-7

Weitere Sprachen	
Russisch in 20 Lektionen	66081-4
Griechisch für den Urlaub*	66699-2
Türkisch für den Urlaub*	66628-6

Allgemein	
Abenteuer Sprache	66936-6

Deutsch	
Fremdwörterlexikon	66446-1
Sag es besser!	66601-4
4000 Sprichwörter und Zitate	66603-0
Zeichensetzung – kurz und bündig	66722-3
Schluß mit typischen Deutsch-Fehlern!	66733-9
Spoiler-Deutsch. Ein Fremdwörtertraining	66798-3
Die neue Rechtschreibung. Alle Regeln auf einen Blick	67084-4

MultiMedia-CD-ROM-Ausgaben

Englisch in 30 Tagen	69051-9
Französisch in 30 Tagen	69052-7
Italienisch in 30 Tagen	69053-5
Spanisch in 30 Tagen	69054-3
Englischer Basiswortschatz	69055-1
Französischer Basiswortschatz	69056-X
Italienischer Basiswortschatz	69057-8
Spanischer Basiswortschatz	69058-6

Die mit * versehenen Sprachentitel gibt es auch als **Cassetten-Packages** (Buch **mit Übungscassette**).

Teste deinen Englisch-Wortschatz

Von Sonia Brough

Sprachen

humboldt-Taschenbuch 723

Die Autorin:
Dr. Sonia Brough war viele Jahre tätig als Lektorin für Anglistik an der Universität sowie als Dozentin in der Erwachsenenbildung und ist nun Verfasserin erfolgreicher Lehrbücher im Fremdsprachenbereich.

Umwelthinweis: gedruckt auf chlorfrei gebleichtem Papier

2., durchgesehene Auflage 1997

Umschlaggestaltung: Wolf Brannasky, München
Umschlagfotos: Walter L. Küchler, München
Zeichnungen im Innenteil: Alfred Taubenberger, Memmingen

© 1994 by Humboldt-Taschenbuchverlag Jacobi KG, München
Druck: Presse-Druck Augsburg
Printed in Germany
ISBN 3-581-66723-1

Inhalt

Vorwort 9

Teil A: Test des Basis-Wortschatzes 11

Übung 1: Vokal-Kuddelmuddel 12

Übung 2: Gegensätze (1) 13

Übung 3: Wortpaare (1) 14

Übung 4: Vergangenheitsformen 14

Übung 5: Verb + Ergänzung 15

Übung 6: Das richtige Wort (1) 16

Übung 7: In der Küche 18

Übung 8: Essen und Trinken 20

Übung 9: Buchstabenquadrat (1) 20

Übung 10: Berufe (1) 21

Übung 11: Wortleiter (1) 22

Übung 12: Präpositionen (1) 22

Übung 13: Substantive (1) 24

Übung 14: Völker und Nationen 25

Übung 15: Definitionen (1) 26

Übung 16: Körperteile (1) 28

Übung 17: Wortgruppen (1) 29

Übung 18: Haus und Wohnung 29

Übung 19: Wortbildung 31

Übung 20: In der Stadt 32

Übung 21: Das fünfte Rad am Wagen 33

Übung 22: Kreuzworträtsel (1) 34

Übung 23:	Urlaub	35
Übung 24:	Die Familie	36
Übung 25:	Obst und Gemüse	37
Übung 26:	Präpositionen (2)	38
Übung 27:	Machen	40
Übung 28:	Gegensätze (2)	41
Übung 29:	Verb + Substantiv (1)	42
Übung 30:	Eigenschaften	42
Übung 31:	Berühmte Gebäude und Stätten	44
Übung 32:	Das richtige Wort (2)	45
Übung 33:	Getränke	46
Übung 34:	Falsch oder richtig?	47
Übung 35:	Berühmte Leute	48
Übung 36:	Wachstum und Fortschritt	49
Übung 37:	Verben (1)	50
Übung 38:	Sammelbegriffe	51
Übung 39:	Sprichwörter	51
Übung 40:	Adjektiv + Substantiv	52
Übung 41:	Pluralformen	52
Übung 42:	Buchstabenquadrat (2)	54
Übung 43:	Aussprache	54
Übung 44:	Im Supermarkt	55
Übung 45:	Die passende Ergänzung	56
Übung 46:	Orts- und Ländernamen	57
Übung 47:	Rechtschreibung	58
Übung 48:	Kalorienkrise	60
Übung 49:	Singular oder Plural?	61
Übung 50:	Satzteile	62
Übung 51:	Substantive (2)	62
Übung 52:	Wortleiter (2)	63
Übung 53:	Berufe (2)	63
Übung 54:	Kreuzworträtsel (2)	64
Übung 55:	Adjektivsteigerung	66

Übung 56: Wortpaare (2) 66
Übung 57: Groß und klein 67
Übung 58: Beziehungen 68
Übung 59: Zeitausdrücke 69
Übung 60: Definitionen (2) 70
Übung 61: Wortreihen 72
Übung 62: Nationalitätsadjektive 72
Übung 63: Verb + Substantiv (2) 74
Übung 64: Präpositionen (3) 74
Übung 65: Gegensätze (3) 76
Übung 66: Verben (2) 77
Übung 67: Das richtige Wort (3) 78
Übung 68: Buchstabenquadrat (3) 80
Übung 69: Wortassoziationen 80
Übung 70: Körperteile (2) 81
Übung 71: Wortleiter (3) 83
Übung 72: Wortgruppen (2) 84
Übung 73: Substantive (3) 84
Übung 74: Falsche Freunde 86
Übung 75: Wortsuche 88

Teil B: Spezialbereiche 91

Übung 76: Geographische Namen (1) 92
Übung 77: Geographische Namen (2) 93
Übung 78: Flugzeuge und Schiffe 94
Übung 79: Fahrzeuge 94
Übung 80: Das Wetter 95
Übung 81: Berufe (3) 97
Übung 82: Ein Dach über dem Kopf 98
Übung 83: Sport 99
Übung 84: Umwelt 100
Übung 85: Spaß am Fliegen 101

Übung 86: Unterhaltungselektronik 103

Übung 87: Arbeitswelt 104

Übung 88: Auf der Straße 105

Übung 89: Krankheiten 107

Übung 90: Im Büro 108

Übung 91: Politik 110

Übung 92: Schule und Ausbildung 111

Übung 93: Geld 112

Übung 94: Amerikanische Ausdrücke (1) 114

Übung 95: Arbeitswerkzeuge 115

Übung 96: Telefonieren 116

Übung 97: Medien 118

Übung 98: Amerikanische Ausdrücke (2) 119

Übung 99: Fotografie 120

Übung 100: Musikinstrumente 122

Schlüssel zu den Übungen 125

Glossar 136

Vorwort

Testen kann auch Spaß machen – das beweist dieser Vokabel-Trainer mit seiner originellen Auswahl an interessanten und lehrreichen Wortschatzübungen. Hundertmal können Sie hier knobeln und kniffeln, und dabei testen, festigen und erweitern Sie Ihren englischen Wortschatz auf abwechslungsreiche und amüsante Art.

Zum Einstieg empfehlen wir Ihnen, ein bißchen zu schmökern. Die Reihenfolge der Übungen ist keineswegs verpflichtend: Sie sollen sich vielmehr die Aufgaben aussuchen, die Ihnen am ehesten zusagen. Achten Sie dabei aber auf die beiden Teile des Buchs: *Teil A* enthält vorwiegend allgemeine Aufgaben, während *Teil B* mit themenbezogenen und etwas anspruchsvolleren Übungen aufwartet. Wir raten Ihnen deshalb, zu Beginn nicht gleich einen Kopfsprung ins tiefe Wasser zu machen. Am besten tauchen Sie zuerst an den seichteren Stellen mal den einen, dann den anderen Zeh ein, bis Sie wissen, wo Sie einsteigen möchten.

Wenn Sie die Übungen durcharbeiten, werden Sie sich nicht nur die geprüften Wörter aneignen, sondern noch einiges mehr: Im Umfeld des getesteten Vokabulars schwimmt nämlich eine Menge zusätzlicher Wortschatz herum, mit dem Sie sich gleichzeitig vertraut machen. Auf diese Weise bewegen Sie sich regelrecht in einem riesigen Sammelbecken englischer Wörter. Damit Sie angesichts dieser Vokabelvielfalt nicht gleich ins Schwimmen kommen, werden schwierigere Ausdrücke am Ende der jeweiligen Übung mit ihrer deutschen Übersetzung angegeben – sozusagen als Rettungsring. Falls Sie darüber hinaus anderen unbekannten Wörtern begegnen, raten wir Ihnen, diese in einem Wörterbuch nachzuschlagen, damit Ihnen der Sinnzusammenhang nicht entgeht. Beim Wortschatzlernen ist nämlich der Kontext wichtig.

Wenn Sie eine Aufgabe bearbeitet haben, können Sie Ihre Antworten mit denen im *Schlüssel* am Ende des Buchs (vgl. Seite 125 ff.) vergleichen. Wir empfehlen Ihnen, die Ausdrücke, die Sie noch nicht kannten, zu notieren (die deutschen Übersetzungen finden Sie im *Glossar* am Ende des Buchs, wo sämtliche Begriffe, die getestet werden, in alphabetischer Reihenfolge aufgeführt sind, vgl. Seite 136 ff.). Versuchen Sie dann, diese Wörter auswendig zu lernen, und wiederholen Sie den Test unmittelbar danach. Am nächsten Tag können Sie den gleichen Test dann noch einmal machen, um zu prüfen, ob Sie den neuen Wortschatz wirklich gemeistert haben. *Wiederholung* ist hier der Schlüssel zum Erfolg! In diesem Zusammenhang noch ein praktischer Tip: Verwenden Sie für Ihre Antworten am besten einen Bleistift, damit Sie die Übungen mehrmals machen können – im Sinn eines Test-Recyclings!

Zuletzt noch ein wichtiger Rat: Auch wenn Sie das Buch mitreißen sollte, Marathonschwimmer sind hier nicht gefragt. Jeden Tag ein paar Längen sind weitaus wirksamer als eine mutige Überquerung des Ärmelkanals. Durch regelmäßiges, konsequentes Üben werden Sie den Kopf ganz sicher über Wasser halten und Ihren englischen Wortschatz Zug um Zug erweitern können.

Wir wünschen Ihnen dabei viel Spaß und Erfolg!

Autorin und Verlag

Teil A:
Test des Basis-Wortschatzes

Übung 1: Vokal-Kuddelmuddel

Zur Einstimmung ein bißchen Denkspaß: In folgender Passage stimmen viele der Vokale (a,e,i,o,u) nicht. Schreiben Sie den Text mit den richtigen Vokalen neu darunter und vergleichen Sie ihn danach mit dem Schlüssel am Ende des Buches (ab Seite 125 ff.).

Congritulotions! You have spont your miney very wosely. As you wark your woy through this beek, you well be amuzed at how quackly your Onglish well imprave. The oxercises are fill of useful vocibuliry which well holp you to spook and write Onglish bitter. Do a few of them ivery doy, and by the tome you have reached the and of the beek you well have a few theesand more wirds at your fungertops. We wash you the bust of lick!

Übung 2: Gegensätze (1)

In dieser Übung geht es darum, jeweils das Wort mit der entgegengesetzten Bedeutung in den Lückentext einzusetzen.
(Eine Hilfestellung bieten die hier aufgelisteten „Schlüssel"-Wörter.)

down	**soft**	**beautiful**
light	**hot**	**boy**
left	**quiet**	**easy**
white	**safe**	**right**

1. This exercise is much too _____ easy _____ (*hard*).

2. It's getting quite _____ hot _____ (*cold*) in here.

3. Try doing it with your _____ left _____ (*right*) hand.

4. I'm going to have the car painted _____ white _____ (*black*).

5. It's quite _____ safe _____ (*dangerous*) to swim off this part of the coast.

6. You've got it _____ right _____ (*wrong*) this time.

7. Our neighbours have just had a baby _____ boy _____ (*girl*).

8. The children were very _____ quiet _____ (*noisy*), as usual.

9. The room at the back is quite _____ light _____ (*dark*).

10. I think their house is _____ beautiful _____ (*ugly*).

11. Mr Fowler lives two floors _____ down _____ (*up*).

12. This boiled egg is too _____ soft _____ (*hard*) for the salad.

13

Übung 3: Wortpaare (1)

Auch Wörter brauchen manchmal Gesellschaft. Welche der folgenden Ausdrücke lassen sich zu einem gängigen Paar verbinden? Schreiben Sie Ihre Antworten in die Kästchen.

1. salt	*and*	**a.** earth
2. bed	*and*	**b.** sour
3. milk	*and*	**c.** breakfast
4. sweet	*and*	**d.** gentlemen
5. TV	*and*	**e.** paper
6. knife	*and*	**f.** death
7. life	*and*	**g.** fork
8. pen	*and*	**h.** sugar
9. ladies	*and*	**i.** radio
10. heaven	*and*	**j.** pepper

1	j

Übung 4: Vergangenheitsformen

Hier geht es darum, die eingeklammerten Verben in die Vergangenheitsform zu setzen.

1. If I had _____ (*know*) they were going to make such a noise, I wouldn't have _____ (*tell*) them to play in the garden.

2. She said she had _____ (*feel*) very hot, but who would have _____ (*think*) it was meningitis?

3. He thinks he's _____ (*grow*) a beard, but it just looks like a bit of fluff to me.

4. Have you _____ (*choose*) a wine yet?

5. Most geese will have _____ (*fly*) south for the winter by now.

6. I haven't _____ (*begin*) to work out how much money we've _____ (*lose*).

7. Tracey has _____ (*spend*) hours looking for her library books, and she still hasn't _____ (*find*) them.

8. What have you _____ (*do*) to your new tie?

9. Oh no, I've _____ (*forget*) to send the Robinsons a Christmas card again.

10. I've _____ (*bring*) you some fresh basil for us to have with the mozzarella.

_____

meningitis – Hirnhautentzündung *fluff* – Flaum **basil** – Basilikum

---

Übung 5: Verb + Ergänzung

Eine der vier Ergänzungen paßt jeweils nicht. Kreuzen Sie die „Betrüger" an.

take
☐ a holiday
☐ a break
☐ a suggestion
☐ some medicine

make
☐ a photo
☐ a noise
☐ a fuss
☐ some tea

complain
☐ about the weather
☐ to the manager
☐ over the cold
☐ all the time

get
☐ wet
☐ blind
☐ rich
☐ lost

do
☐ some work
☐ the ironing
☐ a mistake
☐ sports

go
☐ mad
☐ bad
☐ ill
☐ deaf

Übung 6: Das richtige Wort (1)

Ihre Chancen, hier die richtigen Antworten zu finden, stehen mindestens fifty-fifty. Trotzdem sollten Sie sich in kein blindes Ratespiel stürzen. Versuchen Sie, durch kluges Überlegen den jeweils richtigen Ausdruck in die Lücke einzusetzen.*

1. You look very _____ today. Have you had some good news? (*happy/lucky*)

2. Now that we've got a garden, I'd like to try and grow some tomatoes, onions and _____. (*lettuce/salad*)

3. If you're really worried, make _____ with the doctor. (*an appointment / a date*)

---

* Wenn Sie diese Art von leicht verwechselbaren Wörtern näher studieren wollen, empfehlen wir Ihnen das Humboldt-Taschenbuch Bd. 664, **Schluß mit typischen Englisch-Fehlern!**

4. "_____ makes perfect", as the saying goes. (*exercise/practice*)

5. It's such a lovely day, we're going for a little drive through the _____. (*countryside/landscape*)

6. I'll take our coats to the _____ if you find us some seats. (*cloakroom/wardrobe*)

7. Aren't you children taught to write properly these days? This essay is full of spelling _____. (*faults/mistakes*)

8. Sorry, I didn't _____ this seat had been taken. (*realize/recognize*)

9. Which boarding school do your boys _____? (*go to / visit*)

10. You can't find a place to sit in the park these days with all those tramps occupying the _____. (*banks/benches*)

11. Mr Becket looks quite _____ today – I hope he's all right. (*ill/sick*)

12. A lot of _____ students live in this hall of residence. I always go to their cultural evenings, which are great fun. (*foreign/strange*)

13. Did you _____ (*look/see*) how I changed the baby's nappies? Now you try it.

14. Could you _____ (*remember/remind*) me to switch the answerphone on before we leave the house?

15. When the water has _____ (*boiled/cooked*), you can add the ingredients.

16. Sometimes you can't even get into Mary's bedroom for all the clothes and records lying around on the _____. (*floor/ground*)

17. Well, I don't think much of the _____
(*last/latest*) men's fashions, I must say.

18. That's the last _____ (*game/play*) of chess for
tonight.

19. I keep telling the dogs not to _____ (*lay/lie*) on
the Persian rug, but they just won't listen.

20. When you get off the bus, walk on to the _____
(*nearest/next*) set of traffic lights, and you'll see the fish 'n' chip shop
just across the road on the left.

---

boarding school – Internat   ***tramp*** – Stadtstreicher   ***nappies*** – Windeln
answerphone – Anrufbeantworter   ***ingredients*** – Zutaten

Übung 7: In der Küche

---

*Bevor Mrs Richards auf Geschäftsreise geht, gibt sie ihren Kindern eine
Reihe wichtiger Anweisungen in letzter Minute. Versuchen Sie, die passenden Ausdrücke in die Lücken zu setzen.*

freezer	**washing machine**	**toaster**
coffee-maker	**microwave**	**cooker**
dishwasher	**frying pan**	

Home Alone

"I've left plenty of food for you in the fridge and the _____.

You can use the _____ to defrost and heat up the fro-

zen stuff, but read the instructions on the packets carefully. And don't

forget to clear up after you've eaten. There's no need to use the

_____ unless you've got a lot of dirty dishes. If

you make fried or scrambled eggs, remember to soak the

_____ immediately. And don't forget to switch the _____ off after you've been cooking – we nearly had a fire last time, didn't we?

And do me a favour, please – don't leave all your dirty laundry for me to do when I get back. If you haven't got enough to fill the _____, use the economy cycle. That doesn't waste so much water. Talking of which, could you try to use only filtered water in the _____, please? And if a slice of bread gets stuck in the _____, make sure you unplug it before you start stabbing forks into it. I'd like to find you all alive and well when I get back."

---

defrost – auftauen ***soak*** – einweichen ***favour*** – Gefallen ***laundry*** – Wäsche ***economy cycle*** – Sparprogramm ***unplug*** – den Stecker herausziehen von ***stab*** – stechen

Übung 8: Essen und Trinken

Beim Essen und Trinken muß fein abgestimmt werden. Welche Kombinationen munden am besten?

1.	fish 'n' _____	– *gin*
2.	_____ and eggs	– *butter*
3.	_____ and tonic	– *Yorkshire pudding*
4.	bread and _____	– *ham*
5.	roast beef and _____	– *chips*

Übung 9: Buchstabenquadrat (1)

In folgendem Rechteck sind die englischen Zahlen von eins bis zwölf versteckt. Können Sie sie aufspüren? Suchen Sie von oben nach unten, von links nach rechts, und diagonal in beliebiger Richtung.

o	o	t	e	n	s	g	n
i	n	x	o	i	f	i	n
f	o	u	r	n	i	e	x
s	t	o	s	e	v	e	n
t	w	q	e	e	e	u	r
t	w	e	l	v	e	s	b
d	n	e	e	i	g	h	t
o	t	e	t	h	r	e	e

Übung 10: Berufe (1)

Wer macht was? Setzen Sie jeweils die passende Berufsbezeichnung ein.

1. A _____ flies an aircraft.

2. A _____ delivers mail.

3. A _____ makes people laugh.

4. A _____ treats patients.

5. An _____ works on stage.

6. A _____ drives a tractor.

7. A _____ cooks meals.

8. An _____ writes books.

9. A _____ plays records.

10. A _____ paints rooms.

disc jockey	**postman**	**chef**
author	**doctor**	**decorator**
actress	**clown**	**pilot**
farmer		

Übung 11: Wortleiter (1)

In folgender Wortleiter ändert sich mit jedem Wort ein Buchstabe, bis sich am Schluß das Wort take *in* five *verwandelt hat. Die Definitionen helfen Ihnen, die notwendigen Änderungen zu erraten.*

	T A K E
This _____ is very sweet.	_____
Take _____ of yourself.	_____
A rabbit is different from a _____.	_____
We could always _____ a car.	_____
The _____ spread very quickly.	_____
	F I V E

Übung 12: Präpositionen (1)

Englische Präpositionen sind bekanntlich recht heimtückische kleine Wörter und lassen sich eigentlich nur im Kontext lernen. Bei dieser ersten Präpositionsaufgabe gibt es einen sanften Einstieg: Sie müssen lediglich die richtige Lösung aus den in Klammern angegebenen Alternativen wählen.

1. I've decided to go to work _____ (*by/in/with*) car this morning.

2. My sister and her family live _____ (*at/in/on*) New Zealand.

3. Did you see that cat jump _____ (*up/above/over*) the dog just now?

4. We live quite _____ (*near/nearby/next to*) the shopping centre.

5. I don't like the idea of my mother swimming _____ (*over/along/across*) the Channel in this cold weather.

6. Are you doing anything _____ (*in/on/at*) Sunday afternoon?

7. I like the children to have a lie-down _____ (*in/on/at*) the afternoons – it gives me a chance to read the papers.

8. The pub _____ (*across/opposite/along*) the church is very popular with the staff from the hospital _____ (*down/on/in*) the road.

The pub is very popular with the hospital staff.

9. Your face is absolutely black – go and have a look _____ (*at/in/on*) the mirror.

10. He says he's fallen in love _____ (*in/for/with*) the girl who's just moved in next door.

---

staff – Personal

Übung 13: Substantive (1)

Welcher Begriff umfaßt jeweils folgende Wortreihen?

1. green, red, yellow, Prussian blue *colour*

2. limousine, diesel, coupé, saloon _____

3. oak, pine, cedar, weeping willow _____

4. Alsatian, poodle, terrier _____

5. Rubens, Rembrandt, Turner _____

6. supermarket, florist, butcher's _____

7. Germany, Scotland, Japan, Portugal _____

8. church, house, office block _____

9. measles, polio, scarlet fever _____

10. shirt, dress, socks, skirt _____

11. Beckenbauer, Pelé, Maradona _____

12. whist, bridge, rummy, poker _____

13. Swahili, Dutch, Chinese, Polish _____

14. hockey, baseball, squash, rugby _____

15. Concorde, jumbo jet, Airbus _____

Übung 14: Völker und Nationen

Wer stammt aus welchem Land?

1. A _____ comes from Morocco.

2. A _____ comes from France.

3. An _____ comes from Austria.

4. A _____ comes from Holland.

5. A _____ comes from Spain.

6. A _____ comes from Turkey.

7. A _____ comes from Greece.

8. A _____ comes from New Zealand.

9. A _____ comes from Thailand.

10. A _____ comes from the Philippines.

11. A _____ comes from Germany.

12. A _____ comes from Belgium.

13. An _____ comes from Egypt.

14. A _____ comes from Canada.

15. An _____ comes from America.

16. An _____ comes from Italy.

17. A _____ comes from Hungary.

18. A _____ comes from Cyprus.

19. A _____ comes from Tibet.

20. A _____ comes from Scotland.

Übung 15: Definitionen (1)

Worum geht es in folgenden Sätzen?

1. Some people read one every day.

_____

2. They come in a box and are used to light cigarettes.

_____

3. You need them if you've got bad eyesight.

_____

4. It shows you the route you have to take.

_____

5. You write with it, and it needs regular sharpening.

_____

6. You need it to talk and eat, and you can stick it out.

_____

7. This religious festival is celebrated with eggs.

_____

8. Another word for twelve.

_____

9. If you don't own your flat, you have to pay this.

_____

10. It supplies the power for your radio, dishwasher etc.

_____

11. It is surrounded by the sea.

_____

12. A fruit whose name is also its colour.

_____

13. It allows you to cross a river on foot or by car.

_____

14. Lufthansa and British Airways are well-known ones.

_____

15. What you get on your birthday and at Christmas.

_____

Übung 16: Körperteile (1)

Wo trägt man was?

1. You wear shoes on your _____.
2. You wear a belt around your _____.
3. You wear a beard on your _____.
4. You wear a scarf around your _____.
5. You wear a hat on your _____.
6. You wear gloves on your _____.
7. You wear a ring on your _____.
8. You wear makeup on your _____.
9. You wear a watch on your _____.
10. You wear a cape around your _____.

Übung 17: Wortgruppen (1)

Versuchen Sie, aus folgenden Wörtern vier Listen mit jeweils fünf verwandten Begriffen zu erstellen.

stomach	green	purse	lungs
bank note	liver	monitor	pink
computer	heart	cheque	kidneys
purple	coin	money	hard disk
keyboard	scarlet	floppy disk	grey

_____ _____ _____ _____

_____ _____ _____ _____

_____ _____ _____ _____

_____ _____ _____ _____

_____ _____ _____ _____

Übung 18: Haus und Wohnung

"Home sweet home" lautet ein bekannter englischer Ausdruck, aber nicht immer sieht es zu Hause so rosig aus. Versuchen Sie, die Lücken mit den Wörtern aus dem Kasten zu füllen.

house	**castle**	**flat**	**study**
bathroom	**staircase**	**kitchen**	**roof**
wall	**bedroom**	**living room**	

On the Move

After living in a one-bedroomed _____ for ten years,

I decided it was time to expand. So I moved into a lovely red-

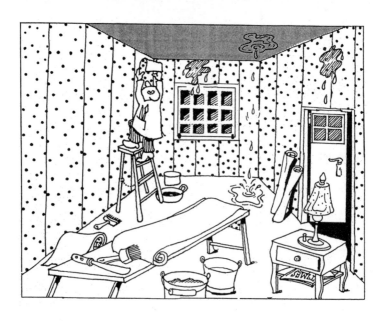

brick _____ in a quiet suburb. Downstairs it has a large _____ with an attractive old fireplace. The _____ faces the back, so that when I'm doing the washing-up I look out into the garden. When you walk into the house, there's a narrow hall with a mahogany _____ that takes you upstairs to the three _____s. As I work from home, I'll be using the biggest of these as my _____. The _____ is a bit tiny, but it's fully tiled and has a power shower. Before moving in, I decided to have the whole house redecorated. Would you believe it, but the day before the big move there was a terrible storm, during which the rain came in through the _____, flooded the loft, and ru-

ined the ceiling and two _____s in the main bedroom.

It's going to cost me a fortune in repairs. They say an Englishman's

home is his _____, but life would certainly be a lot

easier on a royal income.

---

suburb – Vorort   *tiled* – gekachelt   *redecorate* – tapezieren od. streichen
loft – Speicher   *fortune* – Vermögen

Übung 19: Wortbildung

*So wie im Deutschen kann man auch im Englischen – zwar in be-
grenzterem Ausmaß – Wörter zusammenfügen, um neue zu bilden. Versuchen Sie, die Wörter in der linken Spalte mit der jeweiligen Ergänzung in der rechten zu verbinden, und fügen Sie dann die deutsche Übersetzung hinzu.*

thunder	paper	*thunderstorm*	*Gewitter*
team	strap		
news	chair		
watch	dish		
snap	bite		
table	storm		
frost	coat		
arm	cloth		
soap	shot		
rain	work		

Übung 20: In der Stadt

In der Stadt gibt es meistens allerhand zu tun. Wissen Sie, wo Sie hin-müßten, um folgende Besorgungen zu machen?

If you want … you go to the _____

1. a magazine	_____	market
2. a haircut	_____	jeweller's
3. a typewriter ribbon	_____	chemist
4. a dictionary	_____	travel agent's
5. to cash a cheque	_____	baker's
6. a diamond ring	_____	stationer's
7. headache pills	_____	bank
8. to book a holiday	_____	newsagent's
9. petrol	_____	furniture shop
10. fresh vegetables	_____	hairdresser's
11. a bottle of wine	_____	garage
12. a kitchen table	_____	butcher's
13. to borrow a book	_____	bookshop
14. sausages	_____	off-licence
15. some bread rolls	_____	library

Übung 21: Das fünfte Rad am Wagen

Welche Ausdrücke haben sich in folgende Reihen unerlaubterweise eingeschlichen?

1. chocolate, ice cream, onion, toffee, cake

_____

2. grass, moss, blackberry, fern, leaf

_____

3. pencil, ruler, ballpoint, fountain pen, felt pen

_____

4. restaurant, bar, museum, café, coffee-shop

_____

5. horse, rabbit, fly, rhinoceros, lion, giraffe

_____

6. sketch, water-colour, cartoon, paintbox, oil painting

_____

7. circle, square, triangle, pyramid, oval

_____

8. diamond, sapphire, gold, emerald, ruby

_____

9. steak, lamb chop, roast chicken, smoked salmon

_____

10. Asia, Australia, France, Europe, America

_____

11. cricket, tennis, horse-racing, bat, athletics

_____

12. rain, wind, snow, umbrella, sunshine

_____

Übung 22: Kreuzworträtsel (1)

*Zur Abwechslung nun ein kleines Kreuzworträtsel. Fangen Sie an, wo
Sie Lust haben – auch Senkrechtstarter dürfen mitmachen.*

Across

1. He can't even ride a bicycle, never mind drive a _____.

4. I'll have steak _____ chips, please.

6. Have you got any _____ writing paper?

8. She claims she's got nothing to _____ all day.

9. I just can't seem to make my hair _____.

1		2		3
		4	5	
6	7			
8				
	9			

Down

1. It's very _____ in here. Did you turn the heating off?

2. He _____ after the bus, but he still missed it.

3. Five and six don't make twelve – don't they teach you how to _____ at school?

5. The station is quite _____ – it's only ten minutes on foot.

7. The abbreviation of the International Olympic Committee.

Übung 23: Urlaub

Was man nicht alles in den Urlaub mitschleppen muß! Versuchen Sie, folgende Reisebegleiter zu vervollständigen.

1. _ _ _ _ p o r t

2. t r a v e l l e r ' s _ _ _ _ _ _ _

3. g u i d e _ _ _ _

4. _ _ _ g l a s s e s

5. s w i m _ _ _ _

6. v i d e o _ _ _ _ _ _

7. s u n t a n _ _ _ _ _ _

8. _ _ _ _ _ -a i d k i t

9. i n d i g e s t i o n _ _ _ _ _ _ _

10. a d d r e s s _ _ _ _

Übung 24: Die Familie

In folgender Passage tritt ein Großteil der Verwandtschaft der Erzählerin in Erscheinung – da wird es schon manchmal etwas kompliziert. Sie sollen versuchen, die verschiedenen Verwandtschaftsgrade zu erkennen und mit Hilfe der in folgendem Kästchen aufgeführten Wörter den Text richtig zu vervollständigen.

grandfather	niece	cousin	sister
uncle	granddaughter	nephew	grandmother
grandchildren	sister-in-law	daughter	great(...)

All in the Family

I'm Jenny Turner and I come from a big family. I have three brothers and two _____s. My eldest brother's wife is my _____. Their son is my _____.

His name is Daniel, and his sister is my _____. Both

of them are my parents' _____. My father's mother

is my _____, and his father is my _____

_____. I am their _____. My father's brother

Leonard is my _____. He has no children, but my

Aunt Jane has two sons and a _____. They are my

_____s. I could go on. Altogether, there are about

forty-five members of the family, and that's not counting the animals.

When we have a big reunion, my _____-Uncle Joshua

sometimes forgets who are his blood relations and who are the in-laws.

Can you blame him?

_____
reunion – (Familien)Treffen

Übung 25: Obst und Gemüse

Wissen Sie, wie die verschiedenen Obst- und Gemüsearten auf Englisch heißen? In diesem fruchtbaren Unternehmen sollen Sie folgende Auswahl vervollständigen und ins Deutsche übersetzen.

1. c _ r r _ t   **3.** t _ m _ t _

_____   _____

2. a p p _ _   **4.** p o _ a _ o

_____   _____

5. a _ o c _ d o

_____

6. _ r _ n g e

_____

7. c _ b b _ g _

_____

8. g a p _ f _ u i _

_____

9. _ e a

_____

10. m _ n _ a r _ n

_____

11. p l _ m

_____

12. l _ t t u c _

_____

13. b _ _ t r o o t

_____

14. _ a _ a n a

_____

15. k _ w i f r _ _ t

_____

16. g r a _ _

_____

17. o _ _ o n

_____

18. m _ l _ n

_____

Übung 26: Präpositionen (2)

Klein, aber oho! Hier geht es wieder drunter und drüber mit den Verhältniswörtern. Welche Präpositionen fehlen in den folgenden Sätzen?

1. What's _____ TV tonight?

2. I think there's someone _____ the door.

3. Who do you think this poem was written _____?

4. I'd rather live _____ the country than _____ a noisy, dirty city.

5. If you looked where you were going you wouldn't keep stepping _____ the cat.

6. Mind you don't fall out _____ that window!

7. I think he wants to get away – he keeps looking _____ his watch.

8. The girls find it very hard to get out of bed _____ the mornings.

9. We're going _____ the cinema tonight to see Woody Allen's latest film – would you like to come with us?

10. I've spent hours searching _____ my car keys. You haven't seen them anywhere, have you?

11. Sam put his head _____ the balcony railings today and couldn't get it out again. We had to call the fire brigade.

12. What's wrong _____ you, Dad? Have you had some trouble at the office?

13. I'm going to the bank to pay this cheque _____ my account straightaway so that I don't lose any interest on it.

14. Granddad insists on keeping his savings _____ the mattress – he doesn't trust banks.

15. I've just run _____ the park five times, and I'm exhausted.

_____

straightaway – sofort   *exhausted* – erschöpft

Übung 27: Machen

Do, make *oder* take? *Das ist hier die Frage. Vervollständigen Sie die Sätze mit dem richtigen Verb in der passenden Form.*

1. Are you going to _____ the dishes, or are you leaving it to me again?

2. That was a very silly mistake you _____.

3. What on earth are you _____ in there? The noise is dreadful.

4. Could I just _____ one more photo of you?

5. The engine is _____ such a noise, there must be something wrong with it.

6. The whole department has got to _____ overtime this week to get the project finished by the 22nd.

7. He doesn't seem to have _____ any progress since he started at his new school.

8. What are you _____ after work tonight?

9. I'm _____ my final exams in June.

10. How many times do I have to tell you you're not going out until you've _____ your homework!

Übung 28: Gegensätze (2)

Hier geht es darum, die Sätze mit dem Gegensatz des jeweils unter-strichenen Ausdrucks zu ergänzen.

1. Don't <u>push</u> the door, _____ it.

2. If you _____ all your toys on the floor, you'll just have to <u>pick</u> them <u>up</u> again.

3. If I _____ during the meeting, will you make sure I <u>wake up</u> before the director's speech?

4. I asked you a very important <u>question</u>, and I'm still waiting for an

_____.

5. There seems to have been more _____ than <u>peace</u> in this century.

6. Have you checked the <u>departure</u> and _____ times of your train?

7. He has a lot more <u>enemies</u> than _____.

8. I'm afraid this isn't a <u>public</u> park – it's _____ property belonging to Headington House.

9. If I were you I'd put on a <u>thick</u> jumper – you'll freeze in that _____ blouse you're wearing.

10. It's not a <u>lie</u> – it's the _____.

11. One minute he says <u>yes</u>, then he says _____. I don't think he knows what he wants.

12. All the facts you put down must be _____. If you make any <u>false</u> statements, you may be prosecuted.

---

prosecute – strafrechtlich verfolgen

41

Übung 29: Verb + Substantiv (1)

Nicht jedes der Substantive kann das angegebene Verb ergänzen. Streichen Sie jeweils die Ausnahme durch.

1. shut   the door, one's suitcase, the television

2. catch   a ball, a cold, the wind, a thief

3. drive   a bus, a car, a bicycle, a lorry

4. cancel   a flight, an appointment, an aircraft

5. cross   a field, a box, a path, the border

6. take   a tram, a plane, a bus, the railway

Übung 30: Eigenschaften

Zum Glück sind nicht alle Menschen gleich. Versuchen Sie, zu folgenden Sätzen das passende Adjektiv zu finden.

fat	**lazy**	**patient**	**greedy**	**nervous**
generous	**clever**	**cruel**	**honest**	**polite**

1. Mandy just sits around all day doing nothing. She's _____.

2. My brother eats everything he can get his hands on.

He's _____.

3. Jamie came top of the class again. He's _____.

4. How did you manage to bring your children up to be so
_____? Mine have no manners at all.

5. Uncle Nicholas plays cards with the children for hours on end.

He's very _____.

6. The boy next door keeps kicking his dog.

He's so _____.

7. Tommy always shares his sweets with his friends.

He's very _____.

8. My sister weighs too much for her height.

You could say she's _____.

9. Why can't Sean sit still? Is he _____?

10. I would never tell a lie. I'm a very _____ person.

_____

for hours on end – stundenlang

Übung 31: Berühmte Gebäude und Stätten

Manche der folgenden Gebäude und Stätten haben Sie vielleicht schon einmal besucht. Versuchen Sie, ihre Namen zu vervollständigen, und fügen Sie dann in die letzte Spalte den jeweiligen Ort ein, in dem sie sich befinden.

1. Buckingham _____, _____.

2. The White _____, _____.

3. The Houses of _____, _____.

4. Red _____, _____.

5. The Golden Gate _____, _____.

6. The Forbidden _____, _____.

7. The Brandenburg _____, _____.

8. Westminster _____, _____.

9. The Doge's _____, _____.

10. Fifth _____, _____.

11. Piccadilly _____, _____.

12. Wall _____, _____.

Übung 32: Das richtige Wort (2)

Die Qual der Wahl. Hier geht es wieder einmal darum, auf den passenden Ausdruck zu tippen.

1. This box _____ (*retains/contains/entertains*) life-saving medicines.

2. Could you _____ (*tune/tone/turn*) the radio down a bit, please?

3. We'd better be quiet – Kate's _____ (*slumbering / at sleep / asleep*) upstairs.

4. The Harrods _____ (*sell/sale/sales*) starts on Monday.

5. How much did you have to _____ (*purchase/buy/pay*) for those tickets?

6. Chinese is a difficult _____ (*speech/language/lingo*) to learn.

7. They've taken on three new _____ (*male/masculine/man*) teachers.

8. Have you got any ink? My _____ (*pen/pencil/fountain*) has run out.

9. Could you _____ (*signal/sign/signature*) on the dotted line, please.

10. His parents have been _____ (*separated/segregated/divided*) for a year now.

11. I think you should tie that parcel up with a piece of _____

_____ (*ribbon/rope/string*) before you send it back to the factory.

12. What's that _____ (*blot/splash/spot*) on your collar?

---

take on – einstellen   *collar* – Kragen

Übung 33: Getränke

Um welche Getränke geht es im folgenden? Versuchen Sie – Schluck für Schluck – den Definitionen die richtigen Flüssigkeiten zuzuordnen.

beer	**wine**	**champagne**	**tea**
whisky	**cider**	**coffee**	**port**
orange juice	**sparkling wine**		

1. It is said to be a very popular drink in Britain: _____

2. The Turks introduced it into Europe: _____

3. It is made from a citrus fruit: _____

4. It comes from Portugal and is usually drunk after a meal:

   _____

5. It is often drunk on special occasions: _____

6. Apples are the basis of this drink: _____

7. In Bavaria you can drink it by the litre: _____

8. It is made from grapes: _____

9. This drink is also known as Scotch: _____

10. It is bubbly and not too expensive: _____

Übung 34: Falsch oder richtig?

Welche Aussage paßt jeweils nicht zu dem angegebenen Wort?

1. car
   a. It has four tyres.
   b. You fill it up with kerosene.
   c. It has a boot.   _____

2. chocolate
   a. It contains cocoa.
   b. You can buy it in bars.
   c. It has very few calories.   _____

3. aerial
   a. It improves your TV picture.
   b. It can be put up inside or outside.
   c. Insects sometimes have a pair.   _____

4. camel
   a. It has one, two or three humps.
   b. It is sometimes called "Ship of the Desert".
   c. It can live without water ten times longer
          than human beings.   _____

5. soap
   a. You use it to wash yourself.
   b. It melts when you use it.
   c. It is often perfumed.   _____

6. briefcase
   a. It can be made of leather.
   b. You keep it in your inside pocket.
   c. It has a handle.   _____

7. Shakespeare
   a. He wrote plays and poetry.
   b. He won several Oscars.
   c. His first name was William.   _____

8. bank
   a. You sit on it.
   b. There are usually several in the high street.
   c. You can get money there.   _____

9. library
   a. It sells books.
   b. It lends books.
   c. It is usually very quiet inside.   _____

10. photograph
   a. Someone who takes pictures.
   b. Something you can hang on the wall.
   c. Something you can put in an album.   _____

Übung 35: Berühmte Leute

Folgende Berühmtheiten legen Wert auf ihren Titel. Können Sie aushelfen?

Princess	President	Chancellor	Emperor	King
Queen	Admiral	Captain	Pope	Prince

1. _____ Victoria

2. _____ de Gaulle

3. _____ Juan Carlos

4. _____ Rainier

5. _____ Nelson

6. _____ Willy Brandt

7. _____ John Paul II

8. _____ Frederick Barbarossa

9. _____ Cook

10. _____ Caroline

Übung 36: Wachstum und Fortschritt

Wie lautet jeweils die richtige Reihenfolge?

1. adult, teenager, baby, child, toddler

---

2. afternoon, morning, midday, night, evening

---

3. word, letter, sentence, paragraph

---

4. chick, egg, Sunday lunch, chicken

5. town, village, metropolis, city

_____

6. hour, year, week, day, month

_____

Übung 37: Verben (1)

Hier sollen Sie gleich zwei Fliegen mit einer Klappe schlagen. Suchen Sie zu jedem Satz das passende Verb aus dem Kasten heraus, und setzen Sie es dann in die Vergangenheit.

tidy	**do**	**help**	**take**	**write**
make	**wash**	**collapse**	**mow**	**feed**

What did Dad do yesterday?

1. He _____ breakfast for the whole family.

2. He _____ seventeen business letters.

3. He _____ the washing.

4. He _____ the car.

5. He _____ the rabbits.

6. He _____ the dog for a long walk.

7. He _____ the twins with their homework.

8. He _____ up the living room.

9. He _____ the lawn.

10. He _____ in front of the television.

Übung 38: Sammelbegriffe

Welche Sammelbegriffe umfassen folgende Wortgruppen?

1. melon, grapes, lime, pear

2. sonata, concerto, duet, requiem

3. knife, fork, teaspoon, tablespoon

4. table, armchair, bookcase

5. novel, play, biography, poetry

6. pilsener, lager, real ale

7. penguin, eagle, albatross

8. oak, birch, weeping willow

9. trout, salmon, herring, carp

10. spaniel, Alsatian, poodle

Übung 39: Sprichwörter

Können Sie folgende auseinandergerissene englische Sprichwörter wieder zusammenfügen?

1. Sticks and stones may break my bones
2. When the cat's away
3. It's no use crying
4. Barking dogs
5. A bad workman

a. always blames his tools.

b. over spilt milk.

c. seldom bite.

d. the mice will play.

e. but names will never hurt me.

1	2	3	4	5

Übung 40: Adjektiv + Substantiv

Wir wollen wieder einmal unsere Verkupplungskünste verfeinern. Welches Adjektiv paßt am besten zu welchem Substantiv? Fügen Sie Ihre Antworten in die Kästchen ein.

1. windy	**a.** rose
2. high-heeled	**b.** stockings
3. warm	**c.** book
4. tasty	**d.** street
5. illustrated	**e.** weather
6. nylon	**f.** car
7. red	**g.** animal
8. fast	**h.** boots
9. crowded	**i.** welcome
10. furry	**j.** meal

1	*e*

Übung 41: Pluralformen

Wenn Sie zum Beispiel nicht wissen, wie die Mehrzahl von wife *lautet, könnten Sie sich wahrscheinlich nur mit Mühe über Heinrich VIII. unterhalten. Wie viele der folgenden Substantive können Sie im Plural wiedergeben?*

1. wife   _____

2. woman   _____

3. sandwich   _____

4. hero   _____

5. Englishman   _____

6. German _____

7. tooth _____

8. sheep _____

9. lady _____

10. potato _____

11. kilo _____

12. mouse _____

13. child _____

14. house _____

15. foot _____

16. mother-in-law _____

17. leaf _____

18. hobby _____

19. half _____

20. boyfriend _____

Übung 42: Buchstabenquadrat (2)

In folgendem Buchstabenwirrwarr sind zehn Gegenstände aus der Küche versteckt, die Sie finden sollen. Suchen Sie von oben nach unten, von links nach rechts und diagonal in beliebiger Richtung.

p	r	s	p	v	c	r	k	s	s
o	x	h	o	r	r	n	n	l	e
f	l	w	t	g	o	o	i	o	l
r	r	e	n	o	s	u	f	w	m
c	u	i	p	l	a	t	e	a	t
o	n	s	d	b	u	e	w	h	i
o	c	u	p	g	c	h	a	r	l
k	i	l	l	y	e	b	o	w	a
e	n	e	f	o	r	k	o	g	g
r	d	o	p	w	t	b	i	m	e

Übung 43: Aussprache

Der Schein trügt bekanntlich, und dies gilt besonders für englische Rechtschreibung und Aussprache. Wissen Sie, welches Wort sich jeweils nicht mit den anderen reimt?

1. room, tomb, comb, zoom   _____

2. fruit, shoot, put, root   _____

3. through, enough, few, taboo   _____

4. here, appear, fear, pear   _____

5. bed, said, bead, red   _____

6. way, obey, key, delay   _____

7. class, pass, bass, farce   _____

8. goose, lose, juice, loose   _____

9. meet, seat, create, feet   _____

10. palm, jam, lamb, dam   _____

---

tomb – Grab(mal)   *comb* – Kamm   *bead* – Holz-/Glasperle   *delay* – verzögern

Übung 44: Im Supermarkt

Können Sie die Ausdrücke entziffern, die sich hinter den geschüttelten Buchstaben verbergen?

likm   _____

triuf   _____

oiltet repap   _____

eat   _____

posa wopder   _____

oodlens   _____

eesech   _____

scibuits   _____

tubtre   _____

segg   _____

Übung 45: Die passende Ergänzung

Welcher Ausdruck paßt jeweils nicht in folgende Sätze?

1. Our new neighbour is a very... young man.
   a. helpful
   b. intelligent
   c. nuisance
   d. considerate

2. That painting is ... dramatic.
   a. quite
   b. much
   c. incredibly
   d. very

3. Do you read ... novels?
   a. detective
   b. criminal
   c. short
   d. French

4. ... did you do it?
   a. How
   b. When
   c. Why
   d. What

5. I'd rather ...
   a. stay
   b. go
   c. no
   d. not

6. What are you doing ...?
   a. tonight
   b. next Tuesday
   c. last night
   d. tomorrow

7. We mustn't leave the cat ...
   a. outside
   b. home
   c. behind
   d. at home

8. I just want to ... Roger up quickly.
   a. ring
   b. call
   c. shout
   d. phone

9. He … his arm quite badly.

    a. cut   **c.** burnt

    b. hurt   **d.** snipped

10. Mary always arrives …

    a. early   **c.** lately

    b. on time   **d.** in time

Übung 46: Orts- und Ländernamen

Viele Orts- und Ländernamen sind im Englischen anders als im Deutschen. Manchmal sind es nur kleine Unterschiede, gelegentlich scheinen die Namen nichts miteinander zu tun zu haben. Kennen Sie die englischen Entsprechungen folgender Namen?

1. Griechenland   _____

2. München   _____

3. die Türkei   _____

4. Sachsen   _____

5. Rom   _____

6. der Rhein   _____

7. der Schwarzwald   _____

8. Polen   _____

9. Wien   _____

10. Bayern   _____

Übung 47: Rechtschreibung

Die Wortpaare in Klammern haben die gleiche Aussprache, aber ganz verschiedene Bedeutungen. Welches Wort gehört jeweils in die Lücke?

1. Why was Ronald _____ (*scent/sent*) home?

2. I don't even like to _____ (*way/weigh*) myself these days.

3. Do you know the difference between a rabbit and a _____

_____ (*hair/hare*)?

4. I can't _____ (*bare/bear*) him when he's in a bad mood.

5. I feel like _____ (*righting/writing*) to the *Times*.

6. What a _____ (*pair/pear*) of idiots we are.

7. Unfortunately he didn't _____ (*brake/break*) quickly enough and crashed into the car in front.

8. I wonder what it's like being _____ (*air/heir*) to the throne.

9. Did you see that _____ (*dear/deer*) run across the road in front of those cars?

10. I really don't know _____ (*weather/whether*) to send him to his cousins for the summer holidays or not.

11. He says he _____ (*knew/new*) about his promotion six months ago.

12. When we said hello to him, he just _____ (*road/rode*) off on his bicycle.

13. I stood in the _____ (*cue/queue*) for half an hour.

14. How many _____ (*weaks/weeks*) have you been here?

15. My grandfather is gradually losing his _____ (*sight/site*).

16. He keeps all his best wines hidden away in the _____ (*cellar/seller*).

---

in a bad mood – schlechter Laune   *promotion* – Beförderung

Übung 48: Kalorienkrise

Mr Large macht Diät. Wie heißen die Sachen, die er auf jeden Fall vermeiden sollte, und die, die er beliebig genießen darf, auf englisch?

Definitely not:	**As much as you like:**
Schokolade	*Gemüse*
Sahne	*Salzkartoffeln*
Kuchen	*Fisch*
Pommes frites	*grüner Salat*
Spiegeleier	*Obst*
Nüsse	*Mineralwasser*
Salz	*Pilze*
Nudeln	*Tee ohne Zucker*

Übung 49: Singular oder Plural?

Nur eine Alternative ist hier jeweils möglich – mit oder ohne -s*?*

1. Have you heard the latest _____ (*new/news*)?
Roseanne has won the football pools.

2. Mr Baldwin seems to have been losing a lot of _____
_____ (*hair/hairs*) lately.

3. You'd better change your _____ (*trouser/trou-sers*) before you sit down at the table – they're absolutely filthy.

4. I need some _____ (*advice/advices*) on how to
bring up four wild children.

5. Of course you can borrow my _____ (*scis-sor/scissors*) – you don't have to ask.

6. We'd like to express our warm _____ (*thank/thanks*) for everything you've done to help us.

7. Where can I get some _____ (*information/in-formations*) about evening classes?

8. The gardener charges five _____ (*pound/pounds*) an hour.

9. Have you seen my _____ (*pyjama/pyjamas*)
anywhere?

10. Try Maples – they've got a very wide selection of _____
_____ (*furniture/furnitures*).

---

pools – (etwa) Toto   *filthy* – dreckig   *charge* – verlangen

Übung 50: Satzteile

Können Sie die auseinandergerissenen Satzteile wieder zusammenfügen?

1. My father usually	**a.** before I go to sleep.
2. I like to read	**b.** the funniest hats.
3. If it's nice tomorrow	**c.** in a minute.
4. He wears	**d.** seen it before.
5. I've never	**e.** help you with that.
6. All politicians seem	**f.** we'll go to the fair.
7. I've forgotten	**g.** does the cooking.
8. We had to laugh	**h.** to talk too much.
9. I'll be with you	**i.** how to write with a pen.
10. Let me	**j.** when he walked into the lamppost.

1	2	3	4	5	6	7	8	9	10

Übung 51: Substantive (2)

Welches Substantiv verbindet man jeweils mit folgenden Adjektivgruppen?

1. fried, boiled, scrambled, poached _____

2. straight, wavy, curly, grey, greasy _____

3. hot, tasty, three-course, fattening _____

4. fizzy, alcoholic, refreshing, hot _____

5. loud, relaxing, disco, classical _____

6. slow, intercity, high-speed _____

7. expensive, five-star, 20-storey _____

8. German-English, two-volume, pocket _____

9. medium, rare, fillet, grilled _____

10. hard, comfortable, double, guest _____

Übung 52: Wortleiter (2)

In folgender Wortleiter ändert sich in jedem Wort jeweils ein Buchstabe, bis sich am Schluß das Wort name *in* felt *gewandelt hat. Die Definitionen helfen Ihnen, das richtige Wort auf jeder Sprosse zu erraten.*

	N A M E

Shall we have a _____ of cards? _____

A very strong wind. _____

You can get bargains in one. _____

Seawater contains a lot of it. _____

Whisky is made from it. _____

Ice will _____ into water. _____

	F E L T

Übung 53: Berufe (2)

Welche Berufe hatten folgende Berühmtheiten? Fügen Sie den passenden Artikel (a bzw. an) hinzu. In manchen Fällen sind mehrere Antworten möglich.

1. Pablo Picasso   was   _____

2. Marlene Dietrich   was   _____

3. Socrates   was   _____

4. Galilei	was	_____
5. Sherlock Holmes	was	_____
6. Charlie Chaplin	was	_____
7. Heinrich Böll	was	_____
8. Herbert von Karajan	was	_____
9. Andrés Segovia	was	_____
10. Christopher Columbus	was	_____

Übung 54: Kreuzworträtsel (2)

Es geht wieder einmal kreuz und quer. Versuchen Sie, folgendes Kreuzworträtsel zu lösen.

Across

1. Don't get _____ at the Oktoberfest, will you?

5. The opposite of *out*.

6. _____ day I'll be able to speak English properly.

7. The past tense of *fly*.

9. He looked me straight in the _____ and said I was fired.

11. Time for bed – it's getting _____.

14. _____ far, so good.

15. Short for the Metropolitan Opera House in New York.

1	2		3		4
5			6		
7		8			
9				10	
		11	12		13
14			15		

Down

1. It's a hard _____.

2. He's _____ ten, but he talks like an adult.

3. I never thought they would _____ my car away.

4. A _____ model will cost you twice as much.

8. He's as slippery as an _____.

10. *eat* – _____ – *eaten*

12. 7 _____ means seven o'clock in the morning.

13. A popular extraterrestrial being.

---

being – Wesen

Übung 55: Adjektivsteigerung

Versuchen Sie, die Lücken in folgenden Steigerungsreihen richtig zu vervollständigen.

1.	flat		
2.		better	
3.	many		
4.	cool		
5.		worse	worst
6.	thirsty		
7.		narrower	narrowest
8.	difficult		
9.	close		
10.	weak		

Übung 56: Wortpaare (2)

Folgende Wörter warten darauf, sinnvoll gekoppelt zu werden.

1. first-class	**a.** wheel	
2. check-in	**b.** music	
3. precious	**c.** apartment	
4. fashion	**d.** space	
5. steering	**e.** model	
6. newspaper	**f.** desk	
7. pop	**g.** headline	
8. alcohol-free	**h.** metal	
9. top-floor	**i.** beer	
10. parking	**j.** seat	

1	j

Übung 57: Groß und klein

Hier sollen Sie einige „Hierarchien" bilden. Setzen Sie folgende Wortgruppen der Größe nach in die richtige Reihenfolge (von groß bis klein).

1. motorbike, car, tricycle, lorry, van

2. football, marble, golf ball, beach ball

3. tablespoon, teaspoon, soup ladle, gravy spoon

4. snowball, snowman, ice cube, snowflake

5. apple, melon, cherry, plum, mango

6. sea, pond, puddle, lake, raindrop

7. eagle, chicken, blackbird, sparrow, albatross

8. the USA, Canada, Great Britain, Holland, Germany

9. tortoise, mouse, hippopotamus, lion, wolf

10. yacht, battleship, ferry, rowing boat, canoe

---

van – Transporter *marble* – Murmel *soup ladle* – Suppenkelle *gravy spoon* – Soßenlöffel *blackbird* – Amsel *tortoise* – Schildkröte *hippopotamus* – Nilpferd

67

Übung 58: Beziehungen

In folgendem Text kommt eine frustrierte (Groß)mutter zu Worte. Übersetzen Sie die eingeklammerten Wörter ins Englische.

Love and ... marriage?

My Janice has had a steady _____ (*Freund*) for five

years now. They should have been _____ (*verlobt*)

long ago. When I was going out with Arthur back in the fifties, he ask-

ed me to _____ (*heiraten*) him after three weeks.

Within six months we were standing at the altar – it was such a lovely

_____ (*Hochzeit*), I'll never forget it. I just don't un-

derstand the young people these days. They don't seem to want to com-

mit themselves, do they? But I suppose when you see all those

_____ (*geschieden*) couples around, you can almost

understand it. If only my Janice and her Tom would get married, they

could have children and I'd be a _____ (*Oma*) at

last. Life can be quite lonely for a middle-aged _____

(*Hausfrau*) when all the kids have left home. In fact, I think children

have a duty to provide their _____ (*Eltern*)

with _____ (*Enkelkinder*), after all we've done for

them. I can see I'm going to have to have a heart-to-heart talk with

my _____ (*Älteste*) very soon. Or perhaps I could

persuade my future _____ (*Schwiegersohn*) to speed

things up a bit ...

---

long ago – vor langer Zeit, längst   *commit oneself* – sich festlegen   *provide someone with something* – jemanden mit etwas versehen   *heart-to-heart talk* – offene Aussprache   *speed things up a bit* – „ein bißchen Dampf machen"

68

Übung 59: Zeitausdrücke

Hier wird Ihnen die Zeit bestimmt nicht zu lang. Versuchen Sie, den passenden Zeitausdruck in die jeweilige Lücke einzusetzen.

tomorrow	**yesterday**	**today**	**next month**
last week	**last night**	**yesterday evening**	
next week	**Sunday afternoon**	**tonight**	
this morning	**the night before**	**this year**	

1. Is it November already? But that means it's Christmas _____

_____!

2. He's taken his driving test seven times _____, and he still hasn't passed.

3. Believe it or not, I spent the whole of _____, from Monday morning to Sunday evening, spring-cleaning.

4. Patrick just couldn't stop coughing _____. Neither of us got much sleep.

5. _____'s the big day – I've got my interview with the BBC. I think I'd better have an early night for a change.

6. Don't put off until tomorrow what you can do _____ .

7. I've got to have this essay finished by the end of _____

_____, so that gives me exactly ten days in which to do it.

8. What were you doing at 3 o'clock _____ afternoon?

69

9. If you haven't got anything planned for _____,
you can look after the baby while your dad and I go to the theatre.

10. I was surprised at how quickly it got dark _____

_____, and then I remembered that we had put the clocks back

_____.

11. Sorry I'm late for class, but I didn't hear my alarm go off

_____.

12. It was pouring with rain on _____, so they
called the match off.

_____

spring-clean – Frühjahrsputz machen   ***cough*** – husten   ***put off*** – verschieben
call off – absagen

Übung 60: Definitionen (2)

Wovon mag wohl hier die Rede sein?

1. **a.** It is bent.
   b. It turns from green to yellow and then black.
   c. It comes in bunches.

2. **a.** He doesn't say a word.
   b. He is white.
   c. He slowly disappears when the sun comes out.

3. **a.** It is long and thin.
   b. It can be hard to get round your fork.
   c. It is very popular in Italy.

4. a. It sometimes has hands.
   b. It usually goes off in the mornings.
   c. It makes some people groan and turn over.

5. a. It has two covers.
   b. Inside it is often black and white.
   c. It can be opened and closed.

6. a. It comes out of a tube.
   b. Most people use it twice a day.
   c. It has a cleaning effect.

7. a. It is usually square.
   b. You keep it in your pocket.
   c. It is generally made of cotton.

8. a. You can wear it round your neck.
   b. It is sometimes used on a door.
   c. A very heavy one is usually made of iron.

9. a. It has long back legs.
   b. It is often green.
   c. It can swim.

10. a. It contains a lot of knowledge.
   b. It usually comes in several volumes.
   c. Most libraries have at least one.

11. a. It needs a lot of polishing.
   b. It is quite expensive.
   c. Athletes sometimes get it if they come second.

12. a. It's on the roadside.
   b. You wait there.
   c. It usually has a timetable.

Übung 61: Wortreihen

Können Sie folgende Wortreihen richtig vervollständigen?

1. first, _____, third, fourth

2. winter, _____, summer, autumn

3. north, south, _____, west

4. Monday, Tuesday, _____, Thursday, Friday

5. _____, present, future

6. sun, _____ and stars

Übung 62: Nationalitätsadjektive

Mit welchen Nationalitäten verbinden Sie folgende Wortreihen?

1. Alexander the Great, bouzouki, Acropolis

_____ *Greek* _____

2. Kremlin, vodka, samovar

_____

3. pyramids, Pharaoh, Nile

_____

4. Confucius, Yangtze River, Peking duck

_____

5. Samurai, Toyota, harakiri

_____

6. highways, hamburgers, Capitol

_____

7. Versailles, onion soup, Sun King

_____

8. Rolls-Royce, roast beef, Royal Family

_____

9. pasta, Pavarotti, Leaning Tower of Pisa

_____

10. windmills, Rembrandt, tulips

_____

Übung 63: Verb + Substantiv (2)

Welches Verb aus dem Kasten kann jeweils durch die angegebenen Substantive ergänzt werden?

collect	accept	knit	train	count
run	mend	spend	build	tell

1. _____ houses, ships, aircraft

2. _____ money, an offer, the truth

3. _____ numbers, calories, sheep

4. _____ an animal, a team, an employee

5. _____ a story, a joke, a lie

6. _____ a race, a mile, a marathon

7. _____ stamps, coins, postcards

8. _____ time, money, energy

9. _____ a jumper, a scarf, a woolly hat

10. _____ a bicycle, socks, a broken vase

Übung 64: Präpositionen (3)

In folgendem Text fehlen etliche Präpositionen. Versuchen Sie, ihn zu vervollständigen, und achten Sie dabei besonders auf die Ausdrücke aus der Welt der Arbeit.

Work in Progress

I was so fed up with being out of work that one morning I decided to

go back _____ the job centre and accept any work that was

being offered. It so happened that a family was looking _____ an energetic young person to look after their two pet gorillas. Since I had often spent my school holidays working _____ London Zoo, I thought I would be just the right person. But I wasn't the only one. Twenty-seven other unemployed school-leavers had already applied _____ the job. Well, I filled _____ the application form and wondered whether I would hear any more _____ it. Imagine my surprise when I received a phone call _____ the family two days later telling me that I was _____ their short list and asking me if I would come _____ an interview _____ their home _____ South Kensington. When I arrived _____ their house the following afternoon, I couldn't believe my eyes. There were priceless antiques and paintings everywhere, and I saw at least four servants rushing in and _____ of various rooms as I waited _____ the hall. After about ten minutes, I was asked into the magnificent parlour. And there they all were: Mr and Mrs Ponsonby sitting quietly _____ their armchairs while two young gorillas bounced happily _____ and down on the sofas, climbed _____ tables and swung _____ the curtains. Well, I was beginning to have my doubts _____ this particular job and was on the point _____ saying so when both animals suddenly came running up _____ me and jumped into my lap. That settled the matter for my interviewers – they said that their "babies" had never before shown such spontaneous affection _____ a stranger. I was offered the job _____ the spot,

75

and before I knew it I had signed the contract. Oh well, I thought

_____ my way out, it'll be better than an ordinary nine-to-five

job. In fact, by the time I got _____ the gate, I had come to

terms with my future occupation – the servant who had opened the door

for me had just whispered _____ my ear that they used to keep

baby alligators as pets...

---

be fed up – „die Nase voll haben" *out of work* – arbeitslos *school-leaver* – Schulab-
gänger *be on the short list* – in der engeren Wahl sein *priceless* – unschätzbar *parlour*
– Salon *affection* – Zuneigung *nine-to-five job* – geregelte Bürostelle *come to terms
with* – sich abfinden mit

Übung 65: Gegensätze (3)

*Wie lautet das Gegenteil der unterstrichenen Ausdrücke? Fügen Sie die
Antworten in die Lücken ein.*

1. Please <u>sit down</u>. You don't have to _____ every
time I come into the room.

2. If you <u>break</u> that bicycle, you'll have to _____ it.

3. "This bottle of olive oil is nearly _____."
"You'll find a <u>full</u> one in the pantry."

4. I thought you were going to travel <u>light</u>. This suitcase is so

_____ I can hardly lift it.

5. "Do you take _____ photographs?" "No, only
<u>black and white</u>."

6. I think I'll have the <u>sweet</u> and _____ pork for my
main course.

7. "You've <u>put on</u> a lot of weight since I last saw you." "Well, I'm trying hard to _____ it again."

8. This book on economics is so <u>boring</u>. Haven't you got anything more _____ to read?

9. He goes around in such shabby clothes, you'd think he was <u>poor</u>. Yet they say he's the _____est man in the village.

10. "He still seems to be fast <u>asleep</u>." "No I'm not, I'm wide _____ and I've heard every word you've said about me."

---

pantry – Speisekammer   ***shabby*** – abgetragen

Übung 66: Verben (2)

Welche Verben assoziiert man am ehesten mit folgenden Substantiven?

1. pedestrian _____

2. ship _____

3. fish _____

4. mountaineer _____

5. tourist _____

6. soprano _____

7. shopkeeper _____

8. customer _____

9. thief _____

10. bird _____

Übung 67: Das richtige Wort (3)

Die Wörter in Klammern werden oft verwechselt. Versuchen Sie, aus jedem Wortpaar den richtigen Ausdruck auszuwählen.

1. Would you like me to order some food and drink for the first

_____? (*interval/pause*)

2. Our neighbour was arrested for being in possession of a

_____ weapon. (*fatal/lethal*)

3. _____ charges are so high these days, I don't know how some old people can afford to get the medicine they need. (*prescription/recipe*)

4. There's hardly _____ to sit down in here with all this exercise equipment of yours. (*place/room*)

5. My skin is very sensitive to sunlight, so I always try and sit in the

_____. (*shade/shadow*)

6. Paul's busy _____ for his French test tomorrow. (*learning/revising*)

7. I wonder if you could _____ me some cash till Thursday? (*borrow/lend*)

8. I try and _____ the BBC World Service as often as I can – it's an excellent way of keeping up with the English language. (*hear / listen to*)

9. It's such a _____ building that you get a marvellous view of London from the top floor. (*big/tall*)

10. Jennifer's got a new _____. If I was a bit younger, he'd be just the right type for me. (*boyfriend/friend*)

11. Did you _____ (*notice/remark*) how many buttons were missing from his coat?

12. I have to admire her confidence – she's certain that she's going to win first _____ (*price/prize*).

13. Are you nervous about _____ (*passing/taking*) your translator's exam?

14. Mark's ball bounced onto the _____ (*road/street*) and he just ran after it without looking. It's lucky he didn't get

_____ (driven/run) over.

15. I think Laurence Olivier was one of the _____ (*biggest/greatest*) actors of all time.

16. When he _____ (*gets up / stands up*) in the mornings it takes him about an hour before he can even bring himself to smile.

17. She finally found a new _____ (*job/work*) after searching for six months.

18. I don't think that jumper _____ (*fits/suits*) you – you need a stronger colour to go with your pale complexion.

19. Do you think we ought to _____ (*bring/take*) him some flowers or a bottle of wine?

20. Your grandmother's quite _____ (*high/tall*) for a Japanese lady.

---

arrest – verhaften   *be in possession of* – im Besitz sein von   *charge* – Gebühr   *exercise equiment* – Trainingsgeräte

Übung 68: Buchstabenquadrat (3)

Können Sie in folgendem Buchstabenquadrat die zehn versteckten Gegenstände aus dem Badezimmer aufspüren? Suchen Sie von oben nach unten, von links nach rechts, und diagonal in beliebiger Richtung.

f	r	c	t	t	r	p	a	s	t
l	k	a	r	o	a	s	c	i	k
a	n	b	o	o	e	n	h	t	s
n	o	i	s	t	m	t	v	e	p
n	w	n	s	h	a	m	p	o	o
e	u	e	h	b	g	g	s	x	n
l	e	t	i	r	o	t	i	w	g
s	t	a	p	u	e	r	n	z	e
f	a	a	r	s	a	l	k	u	e
w	s	t	s	h	o	w	e	r	p

Übung 69: Wortassoziationen

Welche Ausdrücke assoziieren Sie am ehesten miteinander? Fügen Sie die passenden Wörter der rechten Spalte in die mittlere Spalte ein.

1. grapes	_____	book
2. disease	_____	computer
3. sky	_____	government
4. pilot	_____	hi-fi
5. nationality	_____	goal
6. coal	_____	prison

7. concert	_____	passport
8. music	_____	clouds
9. actor	_____	orchestra
10. football	_____	heat
11. politics	_____	letter
12. crime	_____	medicine
13. disk	_____	theatre
14. pages	_____	flight
15. postage	_____	wine

Übung 70: Körperteile (2)

Wie gut kennen Sie die menschliche Anatomie? Der jeweils richtige Körperteil soll in die Lücken eingesetzt werden.

eyes	**teeth**	**lips**	**mouth**	**neck**
chest	**nose**	**elbows**	**toes**	**arms**
backside	**face**	**feet**	**shoulders**	

1. Sue keeps getting into fights at school. Last time she had two of her

front _____ knocked out.

2. I used to have a lot of freckles on my _____, but they seem to be slowly disappearing.

3. I've got such a stiff _____, I think it must be

from carrying the baby around on my _____ all day.

4. My boyfriend has rather a long _____ and big

ears that stick out, but he has such lovely blue _____ that I fell in love with him straightaway.

5. If you want to get to the front of the queue you'll have to use your _____.

6. I'm so unfit that I can't touch my _____ without bending my knees any more.

7. She looks all right from the front, but it's only when she turns round that you realize what a huge _____ she's got.

8. Your _____ look rather red. Have you been using my lipstick again?

9. My mother has been complaining recently about pains in her _____. We hope she hasn't got heart trouble.

10. He can't dive, so he always jumps in _____ first.

11. I've got long _____, so I find that the sleeves on coats and jackets are usually too short for me.

I think these sleeves are too short for me.

12. Our youngest has got to the age where he'll put anything into his

_____.

_____

freckles – Sommersprossen

Übung 71: Wortleiter (3)

Es darf wieder geknobelt werden. In folgender Wortleiter ändert sich in jedem Wort ein Buchstabe, bis sich am Schluß aus rich *das Wort* bank *ergeben hat. Die Definitionen sollen Ihnen dabei helfen.*

	R I C H
It's mainly eaten in Asia.	_____
That's a very _____ bag you've got.	_____
Four plus five is _____.	_____
I'm afraid there are _____ left.	_____
go – went - _____	_____
It sometimes calls people to dinner.	_____
A group who sometimes cause trouble.	_____
A loud noise.	_____
	B A N K
	_____

Übung 72: Wortgruppen (2)

Aus folgenden Wortlisten lassen sich jeweils vier Gruppen von vier verwandten Wörtern bilden.

playground	chair	magazine	blackboard
brochure	comic	elephant	settee
bear	newspaper	headmaster	crocodile
lesson	cupboard	mouse	table

_____ _____ _____ _____

_____ _____ _____ _____

_____ _____ _____ _____

_____ _____ _____ _____

Übung 73: Substantive (3)

Zwischen Adjektiven, Verben und Substantiven herrschen oft Verwandtschaften. Können Sie aus den eingeklammerten Wörtern das jeweilige Substantiv ableiten?

1. The _____ in this restaurant is very slow. (*serve*)

2. I'm afraid I can't see any _____ of giving you a pay rise. (*possible*)

3. When the headmistress entered the classroom, there was dead

_____. (*silent*)

4. He doesn't show much _____ for his age. (*intelligent*)

5. If you want an exact _____ of the word, you'd better look it up in the dictionary. (*define*)

6. Schoolchildren have to learn to live with _____ from a very early age. (*compete*)

7. His fits of _____ can make life rather difficult at times. (*jealous*)

8. The girl was awarded a _____ medal for saving two young children from drowning. (*brave*)

9. _____ is very hard to find these days. (*perfect*)

10. You'll probably find the _____ in Bombay quite unbearable at first. (*hot*)

11. I can't believe a civilized country like this can have so much _____ in the streets. (*dirty*)

12. The Italian soldiers complained that they weren't given the _____ they had been promised. (*protect*)

13. It was only when I visited East Africa that I understood what _____ really is. (*hungry*)

14. How can you expect to pass your final exams without any _____? (*prepare*)

15. Too much _____ on other people is not always a good thing. (*depend*)

16. His main _____ is that he doesn't pay enough attention in class. (*weak*)

17. She gazed at her new car with great _____. (*proud*)

85

18. What a miserable _____ those refugees must have. (*exist*)

19. The oil spill caused the _____ of thousands of seabirds. (*dead*)

20. It is with great _____ that I have to announce the resignation of our Managing Director, Mr Beeb. (*sad*)

---

fit – Anfall   *drown* – ertrinken   *unbearable* – unausstehlich   *gaze* – blicken   *refugee* – Flüchtling   *oil spill* – Ölkatastrophe   *announce* – bekanntgeben   *resignation* – Rücktritt

---

Übung 74: Falsche Freunde

Nicht alle ähnlich lautenden Wörter in Deutsch und Englisch haben die gleiche Bedeutung. Hier sollen Sie die Wörter in Klammern übersetzen und dabei gut aufpassen, daß Sie nicht in die Falle der „falschen Freunde" hineintapsen. *

1. Some people are saying that the Americans want to _____

_____ (*übernehmen*) the company.

2. This _____ (*Brieftasche*) won't fit into my inside pocket.

3. Have you written your address on the _____ (*Rückseite*) of the envelope?

4. As a teenager he was a very _____ (*sensibel*) lad – you had to be careful what you said to him.

---

* In Band 664 „*Schluß mit typischen Englisch-Fehlern*" aus der Humboldt-Sprachenreihe werden diese „falschen Freunde" ausführlich behandelt.

5. I think it's a _____ (*psychisch*) problem, not a physical one.

6. Don't _____ (*sich wundern*) if you hear the sound of footsteps at night – Raymond sometimes sleepwalks.

7. You don't need to _____ (*Angst haben vor*) the parrot. He always makes a noise when we've got visitors.

8. Could I have that _____ (*Karton*) your new shoes came in?

9. I'm determined to get a better _____ (*Note*) in Biology this term.

10. I don't think I could eat today's _____ (*Menü*).

11. Whenever I go to Belgium, I always have some of their wonderful

_____ (*Pommes frites*) with mayonnaise.

12. The _____ (*Warenhäuser*) are pushing out nearly all the small shops in the high streets.

13. When is flight 709 due to _____ (*starten*)?

14. I must say, your girls are all very _____ (*selbstbewußt*) young ladies.

15. I haven't got the _____ (*Phantasie*) to write children's stories.

16. How much do you think you'll _____ (*bekommen*) for your stamp collection?

17. He's one of the most _____ (*sympathisch*) bureaucrats I've met.

18. When I've finished my _____ (*Studium*), I'm going to spend a year in the Canadian wilderness.

---

lad – Junge   *parrot* – Papagei   *be determined* – (fest) entschlossen sein   *push out* – vertreiben

Übung 75: Wortsuche

Welche Wörter verbergen sich in folgenden Sätzen?
Beispiel: My ear has been hurting quite badly.

1. I'm afraid there's no room in the car for you.

_____

2. I love lychees.

_____

3. Fred ate much too much for breakfast.

_____

4. We live right at the top of the hill.

_____

5. Perhaps I should also apply for his job.

_____

6. If she's back late she'll have to eat her supper cold.

_____

7. I hate asking people favours.

_____

8. Don't drive so fast or else you'll miss the turning.

_____

9. This port tastes very good.

_____

10. They hope radical measures won't be necessary.

_____

Teil B:
Spezialbereiche

Die folgenden Übungen behandeln bestimmte themenbezogene Wortschatzbereiche und sind etwas anspruchsvoller als die in Teil A. Sie sollen Ihnen die Möglichkeit geben, Ihr Vokabular auch im Detail zu erweitern.

Übung 76: Geographische Namen (1)

Wie gut kennen Sie die Welt, in der Sie leben? In folgender Übung soll jeweils das passende Wort aus dem Kasten in die Lücke eingefügt werden. Zunächst geht es ins kühle Naß...

River	Lake	Sea	Ocean	Bay
Falls	Straits	Channel	Delta	Gulf

1. The North _____.

2. The _____ of Biscay.

3. The English _____.

4. The _____ Rhine.

5. The Atlantic _____.

6. _____ Constance.

7. Niagara _____.

8. The Nile _____.

9. The _____ of Mexico.

10. The _____ of Gibraltar.

Übung 77: Geographische Namen (2)

Nach der kalten Dusche in Übung 76 nun zurück auf (größtenteils) festen Boden. Fügen Sie in folgende Sätze die richtige Ergänzung aus dem Kasten ein.

rainforest	**Canyon**	**steppes**	**Peninsula**	**Alps**
Valley	**Forest**	**Desert**	**Mount**	**Mountains**

1. The Sahara _____.

2. The Rocky _____.

3. The Amazon _____.

4. The _____ of Central Asia.

5. Grand _____.

6. The Bavarian _____.

7. The Iberian _____.

8. The Swiss _____.

9. The Rhone _____.

10. _____ Fuji.

Übung 78: Flugzeuge und Schiffe

Folgende Fortbewegungsmittel wären gern in ihrem Element. Können Sie behilflich sein?

ferry	glider	hot-air balloon yacht
speedboat	jet	supersonic aircraft
submarine	steamer	helicopter

AIR   **WATER**

_____   _____

_____   _____

_____   _____

_____   _____

_____   _____

Übung 79: Fahrzeuge

Heutzutage gibt es eine Vielfalt an Fahrzeugen, die sich auf unseren Straßen fortbewegen (oder auch nicht). Erkennen Sie die verschiedenen Fahrzeugtypen?

removal van	motorbike	caravan rickshaw
double-decker bus	truck	tricycle
coupé	bicycle	racing car

1. It has two wheels and can be very noisy.   _____

2. It has two levels and is often red.   _____

3. It sometimes has a total of 20 wheels.   _____

4. It is used for moving furniture. _____

5. It has handlebars and pedals. _____

6. It has handlebars, pedals and 3 wheels. _____

7. It might be found on the Nürburgring. _____

8. It is used for holidays. _____

9. It has two doors and a French name. _____

10. It is a type of Asian bicycle-taxi. _____

Übung 80: Das Wetter

Eines der Lieblingsthemen der Engländer ist bekanntlich das Wetter. Da muß man mithalten können! Welche Wetterbegriffe passen in die jeweiligen Lücken?

snow	**frost**	**lightning**	**puddle**	**wind**
sticky	**ice**	**bright**	**hailstone**	**thunder**

1. Last night's _____ seems to have damaged some of the plants.

2. You can see where that tree was struck by _____.

3. What was that noise? Was it _____ or just another heavy lorry passing?

4. There were very strong _____s blowing during our Channel crossing, and nearly everyone was seasick.

5. I don't mind dry heat, but I can't stand it when it's hot and _____ like this.

6. The clouds will gradually disappear, and it will become _____ and sunny in the afternoon.

7. Please drive carefully – there's _____ on the roads.

8. Well, there's no sign of _____. The children will be disappointed not to get their white Christmas.

The children will be disappointed not to get their white Christmas.

9. I'm not exaggerating – some of the _____s were as big as golf balls.

10. Why do children walk straight through _____s and not around them?

Übung 81: Berufe (3)

Wenn im täglichen Leben etwas schiefgeht, gibt es zum Glück meistens Experten, die einem aus der Patsche helfen. Wer kommt in folgenden Situationen zur Hilfe?

ambulance	**fire brigade**	**gasman**
window cleaner	**doctor**	**electrician**
police	**interior decorator**	

1. If you come home to find someone has broken into your house, you call the _____.

2. If you are running a very high temperature, you should call the

_____.

3. If you want the house redecorated professionally, you call the

_____.

4. If there's a strong smell of gas, you call the _____.

5. If your chimney catches fire, you call the _____.

6. If somebody falls down the stairs and breaks a leg, you call an

_____.

7. If there is an electrical fault somewhere in the house, you call the

_____.

8. If your windows are so dirty that you can't see out of them, you call the _____.

---

chimney – Schornstein   *fault* – Defekt

Übung 82: Ein Dach über dem Kopf

Um welche Bauten geht es im folgenden? Suchen Sie jeweils den passenden Ausdruck aus dem Kasten aus.

mansion	**church**	**mosque**	**cottage**
mud hut	**synagogue**	**semi-detached house**	
igloo	**terraced house**	**skyscraper**	

1. I always feel quite claustrophobic in New York with all those

_____s around.

2. That building over there with the round dome and the crescent on

top is the local _____.

3. A _____ is one of a line of houses that are
joined to each other.

4. Auntie Nell used to live in a lovely little _____
with low ceilings and doorways until she married a very tall man.

5. I can't understand why _____s never melt when
fires are lit inside them.

6. We thought it would be rather nice living next to the village

_____ until we discovered that the bells chime
every hour – day and night.

7. Did you hear about the Senegalese woman in London who got so

fed up with her husband that she built herself a _____
in the garden and moved into it?

98

8. One day I'm going to have enough money to buy myself a great

big _____ in the country surrounded by plenty of land.

9. The old Jewish _____ has just been reopened.

10. Living in a _____ is all right if you get on with
the family next door, though obviously a detached house would be better.

_____

dome – Kuppel *crescent* – Halbmond *chime* – läuten *surrounded by* – umgeben von
get on with – sich verstehen mit *detached house* – alleinstehendes Haus

Übung 83: Sport

*Ohne „Handwerkszeug" läuft nichts. Was brauchen folgende Sportler,
um ihre Sportart ausüben zu können? Schreiben Sie Ihre Antworten in
die Kästchen.*

1. golfer	**a.** horse		
2. footballer	**b.** bow and arrow		
3. cricketer	**c.** oar		
4. show-jumper	**d.** racing car	*4*	*a*
5. water-polo player	**e.** bat		
6. squash player	**f.** club		
7. formula-one driver	**g.** snorkel		
8. diver	**h.** goal		
9. archer	**i.** racket		
10. canoeist	**j.** swimming pool		

Übung 84: Umwelt

Umweltschutz ist ein globales Thema. Deshalb sollte man sich auch in Englisch über die verschiedenen Umweltprobleme äußern können, die unsere Erde heimsuchen. Versuchen Sie, jeweils den richtigen Ausdruck in die Lücken einzufügen.

recycled	**rubbish dump**	**exhaust fumes**	
catalytic	**converter**	**recycling**	**ozone**
waste	**greenhouse**	**cans**	**bank**

1. Do you know if there's a bottle _____ near here?

2. These envelopes are made from _____ paper.

3. Daddy, why hasn't your car got a _____ like everybody else's?

4. Don't throw all those beer _____ into the dust-bin – they can be crushed and reused.

5. The amount of household _____ seems to be increasing all the time.

6. When I step out of the house in the mornings, there's always a strong smell of _____ from the rush-hour traffic.

7. Is it really true that the _____ effect is melting the snow at the North and South Poles?

8. Why don't you give your old furniture to the refugee hostel instead of throwing it onto the _____?

9. The British milk bottle is an early example of _____ .

10. Doesn't it worry you that the _____ hole in the atmosphere is getting bigger and bigger?

Übung 85: Spaß am Fliegen

Heutzutage verbringt man als Flugpassagier oft mehr Zeit am Flughafen als in der Luft. Deshalb an dieser Stelle eine kleine Übung, um Sie mit einigen der wichtigsten Begriffe vertraut zu machen.

departure lounge	**duty-free**	**seatbelt**	**gate**
passport control	**check in**	**runway**	
stopover	**boarding pass**	**hand luggage**	

1. When we got to the airport, it had been temporarily closed down due to repairs to the _____ .

2. You ought to _____ at least an hour before your flight is due to take off.

3. I'm afraid your skis can't go as _____ .

4. Your departure _____ will be announced shortly.

5. These days they usually just wave you through _____ _____ .

6. The _____ was so full that a lot of people had to stand while they waited for their flight to be called.

7. Mr Rumbold spent so much time in the _____ that he nearly missed his flight.

8. They had to provide special _____s for the Sumo wrestlers.

9. It says 9B on my _____ too.

10. We've got two _____s – one in Bangkok and one in Singapore.

---

temporarily – vorübergehend   ***close down*** – schließen

Übung 86: Unterhaltungselektronik

Es ist nicht immer einfach, mit den vielen technologischen Entwick-lungen Schritt zu halten, die allein innerhalb der eigenen vier Wände stattfinden, geschweige denn, sie in einer Fremdsprache zu beschrei-ben. Zum Glück sind aber manche der Begriffe universal, was Ihnen in folgendem Lückentext zugute kommen wird.

CD player	**channel**	**video**	**Walkman**	**gramophone**
satellite dish	**speaker**	**television**	**stereo**	

Sound and Vision

If she isn't watching _____, she's got the _____

_____ on full volume. Now she's not happy with her

scratchy old records any more, so she wants a _____

for her birthday. I keep telling her that CDs are very expensive, but she

says it's worth it because they last forever. She'll be wanting a more

powerful amplifier and big new _____s next. And

that's not all. She's bored with what TV has to offer and says we ought

to put a _____ on the roof to be able to get another

twenty _____s. In fact, you're lucky if you can talk

to her at all these days, because when she isn't glued to the TV or danc-

ing to loud music, she's usually got her _____

plugged into her ears and is totally deaf to the world. Why can't we

bring back the old days when everybody sat around the wireless or _____, and listening to music was a real family experience? Oh, I almost forgot – the new TV soap opera is about to start. I think I'd better record it on the _____ in case it's any good...

---

scratchy – zerkratzt   **be glued to the TV** – vor dem Fernseher hängen (*glued* = angeklebt) **plugged** – eingesteckt   **wireless** – (veraltet für) Radio

Übung 87: Arbeitswelt

Arbeit macht das Leben süß. Können Sie die Lücken in folgenden Sätzen mit den passenden Begriffen füllen?

apply	**pay rise**	**dole money**	**curriculum vitae**
lunch break	**promotion**	**self-employed**	**redundant**
notice	**unemployed**	**job satisfaction**	**interview**

1. If you haven't got a job, you are said to be _____.

2. As compensation you will receive _____.

3. If you see a job advert that interests you, you might decide to _____ for the post.

4. Your job application should include details of your qualifications and work experience. This is usually included in a _____ _____, or CV for short.

5. Your potential employer might ask you to come along for an _____.

104

6. If you prove yourself responsible and efficient, you may be considered for _____ to a higher post.

7. If you feel you can't live off your salary, you can always ask your boss for a _____.

8. Some very busy office workers often work during their _____ _____.

9. More and more people believe that _____ is more important than a high salary.

10. In times of recession, many companies are forced to cut down on their workforce and make people _____.

11. Working from home as a _____ person has its advantages and disadvantages.

12. In most companies, you have to hand in your _____ three months before you leave.

responsible – verantwortungsvoll   *workforce* – Mitarbeiter, Belegschaft   *advantage* – Vorteil

Übung 88: Auf der Straße

Hier geht es darum, die deutschen Wörter in Klammern zu übersetzen. In manchen Sätzen wird Ihnen eine kleine Hilfe geboten.

1. Are you colour-blind? The _____ lights (*Ampel*) were on red, not green.

2. The speed _____ (*Geschwindigkeitsbegrenzung*) in built-up areas is 30 miles an hour, but most drivers seem to ignore it.

105

3. I don't take the car into the city centre any more – there's just too much _____ (*Verkehr*) around.

4. The people in that car don't seem to realize that it's against the law not to wear a <u>seat</u>_____ (*Sicherheitsgurt*).

5. That car with the orange stripes and blue light speeding along the _____ (*Autobahn*) is a police patrol car.

6. Follow the _____ (*Schilder*) to Birmingham, and look out for the Oxford turn-off.

7. Many _____ (*Unfälle*) could be avoided if people didn't drink and drive.

8. In fog you should slow down, switch your <u>head</u>_____ (*Scheinwerfer*) on, and keep a safe distance from the car in front.

9. The big L-plate on the back of the car shows that he's a <u>learner</u> _____ (*Fahrschüler*).

10. If there were more _____ <u>paths</u> (*Fahrradwege*) in this town I might consider leaving my car in the garage more often.

11. I think we ought to cross at the _____ <u>crossing</u> (*Fußgängerübergang*) where it's safe.

12. We've been stuck behind that line of lorries for ages, but I just can't see far enough to _____ (*überholen*).

Übung 89: Krankheiten

Wie steht es mit Ihrer diagnostischen Begabung? Versuchen Sie, die Sätze mit dem jeweils richtigen Begriff aus dem Kasten zu vervollständigen.

measles	backache	stomach-ache	sore throat
cold	temperature	allergic	rheumatism
flu	appendicitis		

1. Terry's been sneezing. I hope he isn't getting a _____.

2. My sister loves furry animals, but she's _____ to them.

3. Does your husband also suddenly get a _____ when you ask him to do the gardening?

4. Hot milk and honey will soothe your _____.

5. There's a terrible _____ virus going round. Most of the department have been off work this week.

6. The _____ in my joints always gets worse when the weather changes.

7. Can you remember whether you had _____ as a child?

8. I thought it was a case of severe indigestion, but it turned out to be

_____ and I had to be taken to hospital.

107

9. The baby feels quite hot – I think she might be running a

_____.

10. I'm not surprised you've got a _____ after eating all those sweets and chocolates.

_____

sneeze – niesen *furry animal* – Pelztier *soothe* – lindern *joints* – Gelenke
indigestion – Magenverstimmung

Übung 90: Im Büro

Und nun ein kleiner Test für Büromenschen. Welches Wort gehört in welche Lücke?

envelope	**typewriter**	**desk**	**typing error**
staple	**ruler**	**boss**	
diary	**screen**	**tea break**	

1. Most secretaries these days tend to use either electronic

_____s or word processors.

2. These lines aren't straight. Haven't you got a _____ ?

3. Fred just can't adapt to the new office technology – he still sometimes puts Tippex on the computer _____ when he makes a mistake.

4. Is that a dog you're hiding under your _____, Mr Baker?

What's that funny noise, Mr Baker?

5. I think the _____s in this company are much too short.

6. I've arranged to see Dr Shaw on Wednesday at 2 p.m. Could you put that in the _____, please?

7. Put those comics away, quick! Here comes the _____!

8. Gladys, can you please explain why this letter you retyped still has the wrong date and several _____s?

9. Could you make ten copies of this report, _____ them together and have them ready in time for the meeting at two o'clock, please.

10. Can you spare me a couple of your big brown padded _____s?

Übung 91: Politik

Wie lauten die vollständigen Bezeichnungen aus der Politikszene Großbritanniens?

1. _____ Minister (*Premierminister*)

2. _____ of the Exchequer (*Schatzkanzler*)

3. _____ Secretary (*Außenminister*)

4. _____ Secretary (*Innenminister*)

5. _____ Cabinet (*Schattenkabinett*)

6. House of _____ (*Unterhaus*)

7. _____ Speaker (*etwa: Herr Präsident*)

8. _____ Speaker (*etwa: Frau Präsidentin*)

9. Question _____ (*Fragestunde*)

10. _____ of the Opposition (*Oppositionsführer*)

Übung 92: Schule und Ausbildung

Zeit zum Büffeln. Welche Ausdrücke passen in welche Lücken?

library	homework	exercise	subject
pupil	course	school	exam
teacher	qualification	University	class

1. He says he's too busy revising for his Geography _____, but I think it's just an excuse.

2. Some children in Britain start _____ at the age of four.

3. Our eldest daughter is studying history and French at London

_____.

4. Afternoon _____es start at two o'clock.

5. I'm a physics _____ at a comprehensive school in Manchester.

6. Which _____ do you prefer, biology or maths?

7. You'll probably find her in the _____ writing her essay.

8. I can't decide whether to take a _____ in business studies or classics.

9. How many _____s are there in your class?

10. I don't feel like doing _____ any more – I'm going round to play computer games with Mandy.

11. This book of English vocabulary _____s is the best.

12. He left school without any _____s, but that didn't stop him having a successful career and getting very rich.

classics – Altphilologie

Übung 93: Geld

Hier haben Sie es wieder mit einem ganz wichtigen Thema zu tun. Deshalb ein kleiner Test, um zu sehen, wie „solvent" Sie in diesem Wortschatzbereich sind.

account	**interest**	**currency**	**pocket money**	
cash dispenser	**spend**	**credit card**	**debt**	**change**
cheque	**piggy bank**		**coin**	**pound**

Money makes the world go round

I'll never forget my sixteenth birthday – that was when my father gave

me a _____ for £100 so that I could open my own

bank _____. After years of dropping ten- and fifty-

pence _____s into a blue and white porcelain

_____, I could finally invest my money with a bank

and start earning _____.

Then came the age of the _____ – that won-

derful hole in the wall which allows you to withdraw money any time

of the day or night. I decided to make life even easier for myself by ap-

plying for a _____. Within a year I had eight of them.

It made going abroad on holiday so easy – I didn't have to worry about

going to the bank and buying lots of foreign _____

any more. A bit of small _____ in my pocket was all

I needed – my plastic cards would see to the rest. I felt I could

_____ money whenever I felt like it.

Well, it was nice while it lasted. Now I long for the innocent days of

money boxes, when I would look after the weekly _____.
Dad gave me as if it was pure gold. I'm in prison, you see, serving a
three-year sentence for not paying off my _____s.
It's funny, but as I gaze through the window of my cell, my father's
words keep coming back to me: "Look after the pennies, son," he used
to say, "and the _____s will look after themselves."
I must admit he was right about that. Well, I must rush off to the games
room now – our evening roulette session starts in two minutes…

---

withdraw – abheben   ***long for*** – sich sehnen nach   ***sentence*** – Strafe

Übung 94: Amerikanische Ausdrücke (1)

In dieser Ära der regen transatlantischen Kommunikation ist es besonders nützlich, sich mit einigen der Unterschiede zwischen dem britischen und amerikanischen Wortschatz vertraut zu machen. In dieser Aufgabe sollen Sie die englische Entsprechung und die deutsche Übersetzung des jeweils unterstrichenen amerikanischen Wortes liefern.

z. B . A new movie theater has just opened in town.

   cinema   *Kino*

1. I think the kids must have been eating cookies again – the carpet's covered in crumbs.

_____   _____

2. Waiter, could I have the check, please?

_____   _____

3. You'll find that gas is cheaper in the United States than in Europe.

_____   _____

4. They say it's dangerous to use the subway at night.

_____   _____

5. The lift got stuck between the first floor and the second floor.

_____   _____

_____   _____

6. You see so many people begging on the sidewalk these days, it's quite depressing.

_____   _____

7. Have you got a schedule of Lufthansa flights to Europe?

_____   _____

8. There's a <u>package</u> for you in the hall.

_____   _____

9. The <u>rest rooms</u> are downstairs.

_____   _____

10. I hardly slept at all – the <u>faucet</u> was dripping all night long.

_____   _____

_____

beg – betteln

Übung 95: Arbeitswerkzeuge

Wer braucht was? Setzen Sie die passenden Werkzeuge aus der mittleren Spalte zu den Berufsbezeichnungen links.

1. architect	**a.** saw		
2. TV announcer	**b.** spade		
3. writer	**c.** space suit		
4. hairdresser	**d.** oven		
5. sculptor	**e.** ladder		
6. cook	**f.** microscope		
7. policeman	**g.** drill		
8. cab driver	**h.** drawing board		
9. gardener	**i.** needle		
10. biochemist	**j.** microphone		
11. carpenter	**k.** taxi		
12. chimney-sweep	**l.** patrol car		
13. photographer	**m.** calculator		
14. nurse	**n.** word processor	*14*	*i*
15. dentist	**o.** helmet		
16. astronaut	**p.** scissors		
17. fireman	**q.** chisel		
18. accountant	**r.** camera		

Übung 96: Telefonieren

Was wäre das moderne Leben ohne das Telefon? Um für die interna-tionale Kommunikation ein wenig ausgerüstet zu sein, sollten Sie sich einige telefonische Grundbegriffe aus dem Englischen angeeignet haben. Den richtigen Ausdruck setzen Sie bitte in die entsprechende Lücke.

phone box	**dial**	**long-distance**	**operator**
telephone directory		**answerphone**	**phonecard**
cordless phone	**switchboard**		**yellow pages**

1. These days, many people prefer to use _____s rather than coins.

2. With my arthritis, I find it much easier using these modern phones

than having to _____ numbers on the old-fashioned phones.

3. I can't understand why those lovely old red _____

_____es have been replaced by the ugly things you see these days.

4. If you didn't make so many _____ phone calls in the middle of the day, our phone bill wouldn't be so high.

5. This _____ is three years old – no wonder I can't find her number in it.

6. This is the fourth time I've been cut off on the phone this morning.

I think I'd better ring the _____.

7. If you're running your own business, you can have the company

name and number published in the _____ free of charge.

8. The company gets so many phone calls that they now employ five

_____ operators.

9. She keeps complaining that my _____ doesn't leave enough time for her to record her messages.

10. What you need is a _____ which you can take into the garden with you.

---

be cut off – unterbrochen werden

Übung 97: Medien

Der vorletzte Lückentest in diesem Buch. Versuchen Sie, die Sätze mit den Wörtern aus dem Kasten zu vervollständigen.

headline	**newspaper**	**journalist**	**editor**
newsreader	**press**	**article**	**censorship**
TV	**circulation**	**magazine**	

1. Freedom of the _____ is one of the fundamental rights of a democratic society.

2. What I really hate about _____ is the fact that they keep interrupting programmes with adverts.

3. Do you read a local _____?

4. He started out as a sports _____, and now he's

_____ of a national paper.

5. Some of the _____s on TV have rather strange hairstyles.

6. I don't believe in _____, but I feel something should be done to encourage newspapers to respect people's privacy.

7. You find a lot of clever wordplay in the _____s of British newspapers.

8. She says she can't afford to feed her three children, but it doesn't

stop her from buying lots of expensive glossy _____s.

9. Publishing all these scandals about politicians and royals is just an

attempt to increase _____ figures.

10. Did you read the leading _____ in today's *Independent* on the future of broadcasting?

---

interrupt – unterbrechen   *wordplay* – Wortspiele   *broadcasting* – Rundfunk und Fernsehen

Übung 98: Amerikanische Ausdrücke (2)

In dieser Aufgabe können Sie sowohl Ihren britischen als auch Ihren amerikanischen Wortschatz testen. Es wird lediglich der deutsche Ausdruck angegeben: Sie sollen die britischen und amerikanischen Entsprechungen vervollständigen.

	britisch	amerikanisch
1. Wohnung		
2. dritter Stock		
3. Entschuldigung!		
4. Herbst		
5. Briefkasten		
6. Urlaub		
7. Aufzug		
8. Taschenlampe		
9. Kino		
10. Handtasche		
11. Hose		
12. Pommes frites		
13. Autobahn		
14. Geschäft		
15. Bonbon		
16. Marmelade		
17. Führerschein		
18. Abfall		
19. Kofferraum		
20. Geldschein		

Übung 99: Fotografie

Bitte lächeln, denn hier geht es um ein weitverbreitetes Hobby: das Fotografieren. Hoffentlich sind Sie für diesen Test noch aufnahmefähig. Die deutschen Ausdrücke in Klammern warten darauf, übersetzt zu werden, aber um Sie bei diesem etwas technischen Thema nicht völlig im Stich zu lassen, haben wir die englischen Begriffe im Kasten angegeben.

equipment	shots	wide-angle	slide
telephoto	photographer	screen	tripod
accessories	flashlight	lenses	prints

Camera shy?

I'm quite a keen _____ (*Fotograf*), so I always take

my camera _____ (*Ausrüstung*) with me when I go

abroad. I have two camera bodies and four _____

120

(*Objektive*), including a _____ (*Weitwinkel ...*) lens for architectural _____ (*Aufnahmen*) or landscapes and a _____ (*Tele*) for close-ups of people or animals. Then there's my _____ (*Stativ*) to keep the camera steady if I'm taking photos indoors or at night, plus lots of filters and other bits and pieces. Occasionally I will use a _____ _____ (*Blitzlicht*), but I try and take photos in natural light whenever possible. Personally I prefer _____ (*Dia ...*) film to negatives, although I usually have _____ (*Abzüge*) made of the best photos. In my opinion, there's nothing better than seeing holiday snaps projected onto a big _____ (*Leinwand*). I'm afraid my husband doesn't share my photographic enthusiasm – he keeps trying to persuade me to get rid of all my cameras and _____ (*Zubehör*) and get one of those new, fully automatic cameras. I just think it's because he doesn't like carrying my camera gear around for me whenever we go on holiday.

---

steady – ruhig   *snaps* – Schnappschüsse   *persuade* – überreden   *camera gear* – Kameraausrüstung

Übung 100: Musikinstrumente

Zur allerletzten Aufgabe etwas Musik. Auch wenn Sie sie nicht spielen können ... können Sie die folgenden Musikinstrumente vervollständigen?

1. Louis Armstrong played it.

_ r _ _ _ _ t

2. It has black and white keys and three feet.

g _ _ _ _   p _ _ _ _

3. It is a popular jazz wind instrument.

_ _ x _ p _ _ _ _

4. You bang them together to make a sound.

c _ _ b _ _ _

5. Most western churches have one.

_ _ g _ _

6. It has four strings and is often played in rock bands.

_ a _ _   g _ _ _ _ _

7. It is usually taller than the player.

d _ _ _ _ _   _ _ s s

8. We generally associate them with Scotland.

_ _ g p _ _ _ _

9. It has a keyboard on either side and bellows.

_ c c _ _ _ _ _ _

10. You have to blow and suck to play it.

_ _ _ t h   o _ _ _ _

11. You play it with a bow.

_ _ _ _ i n

12. It's a wind instrument which makes a very deep sound.

b _ s _ _ _ n

13. You beat them with sticks.

_ r _ _ _

14. They are often used in flamenco dancing.

_ _ s t _ n _ _ _

15. It is an old instrument related to the piano.

h _ _ _ s _ c h _ _ _

---

bellows – Balg

Schlüssel zu den Übungen

Teil A

Übung 1: Congratulations! You have spent your money very wisely. As you work your way through this book, you will be amazed at how quickly your English will improve. The exercises are full of useful vocabulary which will help you to speak and write English better. Do a few of them every day, and by the time you have reached the end of the book you will have a few thousand more words at your fingertips. We wish you the best of luck!

Übung 2: **1.** easy **2.** hot **3.** left **4.** white **5.** safe **6.** right **7.** boy **8.** quiet **9.** light **10.** beautiful **11.** down **12.** soft

Übung 3: 1j / 2c / 3h / 4b / 5i / 6g / 7f / 8e / 9d / 10a

Übung 4: **1.** known; told **2.** felt; thought **3.** grown **4.** chosen **5.** flown **6.** begun; lost **7.** spent; found **8.** done **9.** forgotten **10.** brought

Übung 5: **take** a suggestion (*richtig:* make a suggestion) / **make** a photo (*richtig:* take a photo) / **complain** over the cold (*richtig:* complain about the cold) / **get** blind (*richtig:* go blind) / **do** a mistake (*richtig:* make a mistake) / **go** ill (*richtig:* fall/become ill)

Übung 6: **1.** happy **2.** lettuce **3.** an appointment **4.** practice **5.** countryside **6.** cloakroom **7.** mistakes **8.** realize **9.** go to **10.** benches **11.** ill **12.** foreign **13.** see **14.** remind **15.** boiled **16.** floor **17.** latest **18.** game **19.** lie **20.** next

Übung 7: the fridge and the **freezer** / use the **microwave** to defrost / no need to use the **dishwasher** / soak the **frying pan** / switch the **cooker** off / fill the **washing machine** / filtered water in the **coffee-maker** / gets stuck in the **toaster**

Übung 8: 1. chips **2.** ham **3.** gin **4.** butter **5.** Yorkshire pudding

Übung 9:

o	o	t	e	n	s	g	n
i	n	x	o	i	f	i	n
f	o	u	r	n	i	e	x
s	t	o	s	e	v	e	n
t	w	q	e	e	e	u	r
t	w	e	l	v	e	s	b
d	n	e	e	i	g	h	t
o	t	e	t	h	r	e	e

Übung 10: **1.** pilot **2.** postman **3.** clown **4.** doctor **5.** actress **6.** farmer **7.** chef **8.** author **9.** disc jockey **10.** decorator

Übung 11: **TAKE**, CAKE, CARE, HARE, HIRE, FIRE, **FIVE**

Übung 12: **1.** by **2.** in **3.** over **4.** near **5.** across **6.** on **7.** in **8.** opposite; down **9.** in **10.** with

Übung 13: **1.** colour **2.** car **3.** tree **4.** dog **5.** painter/artist **6.** shop **7.** country **8.** building **9.** illness/disease **10.** clothes/clothing **11.** footballer / soccer player **12.** card game **13.** (foreign) language **14.** sport / ball game **15.** aeroplane/aircraft

Übung 14: **1.** Moroccan **2.** Frenchman/Frenchwoman **3.** Austrian **4.** Dutchman/Dutchwoman **5.** Spaniard **6.** Turk **7.** Greek **8.** New Zealander **9.** Thai **10.** Filipino **11.** German **12.** Belgian **13.** Egyptian **14.** Canadian **15.** American **16.** Italian **17.** Hungarian **18.** Cypriot **19.** Tibetan **20.** Scot/Scotsman/Scotswoman

Übung 15: **1.** newspaper **2.** matches **3.** glasses/spectacles **4.** map **5.** pencil **6.** tongue **7.** Easter **8.** dozen **9.** rent **10.** electricity **11.** island **12.** orange **13.** bridge **14.** airlines **15.** present(s)

Übung 16: **1.** feet **2.** waist **3.** chin **4.** neck **5.** head **6.** hands **7.** finger **8.** face **9.** wrist **10.** shoulders

Übung 17:

stomach	green	purse	monitor
lungs	purple	bank note	computer
liver	scarlet	coin	hard disk
heart	grey	money	keyboard
kidneys	pink	cheque	floppy disk

Übung 18: one-bedroomed **flat** / red-brick **house** / a large **living room** / The **kitchen** faces / mahogany **staircase** / the three **bedroom**s / as my **study** / The **bathroom** is a bit tiny / through the **roof** / two **wall**s / home is his **castle**

Übung 19: thunderstorm - *Gewitter* / teamwork – *Teamarbeit* / newspaper – *Zeitung* / watchstrap – *Uhrarmband* / snapshot – *Schnappschuß* / tablecloth – *Tischdecke* / frostbite – *Erfrierungen* / armchair – *Sessel* / soapdish – *Seifenschale* / raincoat – *Regenmantel*

Übung 20: **1.** newsagent's **2.** hairdresser's **3.** stationer's **4.** bookshop **5.** bank **6.** jeweller's **7.** chemist **8.** travel agent's **9.** garage **10.** market **11.** off-licence **12.** furniture shop **13.** library **14.** butcher's **15.** baker's

Übung 21: **1.** onion **2.** blackberry **3.** ruler **4.** museum **5.** fly **6.** paintbox **7.** pyramid **8.** gold **9.** smoked salmon **10.** France **11.** bat **12.** umbrella

Übung 22:

1 C	A	2 R		3 A
O		4 A	5 N	D
6 L	7 I	N	E	D
8 D	O		A	
	9 C	U	R	L

Übung 23: **1.** passport **2.** traveller's cheques **3.** guidebook **4.** sunglasses **5.** swimsuit **6.** video camera **7.** suntan lotion **8.** first-aid kit **9.** indigestion tablets **10.** address book

Übung 24: two **sister**s / is my **sister-in-law** / Their son is my **nephew** / his sister is my **niece** / my parents' **grandchildren** / my **grandmother** / my **grandfather** / their **granddaughter** / Leonard is my **uncle** / two sons and a **daughter** / my **cousin**s / my **Great**-Uncle Joshua

Übung 25: **1.** carrot **2.** apple **3.** tomato **4.** potato **5.** avocado **6.** orange **7.** cabbage **8.** grapefruit **9.** pea **10.** mandarin **11.** plum **12.** lettuce **13.** beetroot **14.** banana **15.** kiwifruit **16.** grape **17.** onion **18.** melon

| **Übung 26:** | **1.** on **2.** at **3.** by **4.** in; in **5.** on **6.** of **7.** at **8.** in **9.** to **10.** for **11.** through **12.** with **13.** into **14.** under **15.** (a)round

| **Übung 27:** | **1.** do **2.** made **3.** doing **4.** take **5.** making **6.** do **7.** made **8.** doing **9.** taking / (*seltener*) doing **10.** done

| **Übung 28:** | **1.** pull **2.** drop **3.** fall asleep **4.** answer **5.** war **6.** arrival **7.** friends **8.** private **9.** thin **10.** truth **11.** no **12.** correct

| **Übung 29:** | **1.** the television **2.** the wind **3.** a bicycle **4.** an aircraft **5.** a box **6.** the railway

| **Übung 30:** | **1.** lazy **2.** greedy **3.** clever **4.** polite **5.** patient **6.** cruel **7.** generous **8.** fat **9.** nervous **10.** honest

| **Übung 31:** | **1.** Buckingham **Palace, London** **2.** The White **House, Washington** **3.** The Houses of **Parliament, London** **4.** Red **Square, Moscow** **5.** The Golden Gate **Bridge, San Francisco** **6.** The Forbidden **City, Peking/Beijing** **7.** The Brandenburg **Gate, Berlin** **8.** Westminster **Bridge, London** **9.** The Doge's **Palace, Venice** **10.** Fifth **Avenue, New York** **11.** Piccadilly **Circus, London** **12.** Wall **Street, New York**

| **Übung 32:** | **1.** contains **2.** turn **3.** asleep **4.** sale **5.** pay **6.** language **7.** male **8.** pen **9.** sign **10.** separated **11.** string **12.** spot

| **Übung 33:** | **1.** tea **2.** coffee **3.** orange juice **4.** port **5.** champagne **6.** cider **7.** beer **8.** wine **9.** whisky **10.** sparkling wine

| **Übung 34:** | 1b / 2c / 3c / 4a / 5b / 6b / 7b / 8a / 9a / 10a

| **Übung 35:** | **1. Queen** Victoria **2. President** de Gaulle **3. King** Juan Carlos **4. Prince** Rainier **5. Admiral** Nelson **6. Chancellor** Willy Brandt **7. Pope** John Paul II **8. Emperor** Frederick Barbarossa **9. Captain** Cook **10. Princess** Caroline

| **Übung 36:** | **1.** baby, toddler, child, teenager, adult **2.** morning, midday, afternoon, evening, night **3.** letter, word, sentence, paragraph **4.** egg, chick, chicken, Sunday lunch **5.** village, town, city, metropolis **6.** hour, day, week, month, year

| **Übung 37:** | **1.** made **2.** wrote **3.** did **4.** washed **5.** fed **6.** took **7.** helped **8.** tidied **9.** mowed **10.** collapsed

Übung 38: 1. fruit(s) 2. music 3. cutlery 4. furniture 5. literature 6. beer(s) 7. bird(s) 8. tree(s) 9. fish 10. dog(s)

Übung 39: 1e / 2d / 3b / 4c / 5a

Übung 40: 1e / 2h / 3i / 4j / 5c / 6b / 7a / 8f / 9d / 10g

Übung 41: 1. wives 2. women 3. sandwiches 4. heroes 5. Englishmen 6. Germans 7. teeth 8. sheep 9. ladies 10. potatoes 11. kilos 12. mice 13. children 14. houses 15. feet 16. mothers-in-law 17. leaves 18. hobbies 19. halves 20. boyfriends

Übung 42:

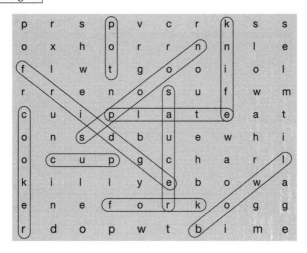

Übung 43: 1. comb 2. put 3. enough 4. pear 5. bead 6. key 7. bass 8. lose 9. create 10. palm

Übung 44: milk / fruit / toilet paper / tea / soap powder / noodles / cheese / biscuits / butter / eggs

Übung 45: 1c / 2b / 3b / 4d / 5c / 6c / 7b / 8c / 9d / 10c

Übung 46: 1. Greece 2. Munich 3. Turkey 4. Saxony 5. Rome 6. the Rhine 7. the Black Forest 8. Poland 9. Vienna 10. Bavaria

Übung 47: **1.** sent **2.** weigh **3.** hare **4.** bear **5.** writing **6.** pair **7.** brake **8.** heir **9.** deer **10.** whether **11.** knew **12.** rode **13.** queue **14.** weeks **15.** sight **16.** cellar

Übung 48: **Definitely not:** chocolate / cream / cake / chips / fried eggs / nuts / salt / noodles/pasta
As much as you like: vegetables / boiled potatoes / fish / lettuce / fruit / mineral water / mushrooms / tea without sugar

Übung 49: **1.** news **2.** hair **3.** trousers **4.** advice **5.** scissors **6.** thanks **7.** information **8.** pounds **9.** pyjamas **10.** furniture

Übung 50: 1g / 2a / 3f / 4b / 5d / 6h / 7i / 8j / 9c / 10e

Übung 51: **1.** egg(s) **2.** hair **3.** meal **4.** drink **5.** music **6.** train **7.** hotel **8.** dictionary **9.** steak **10.** bed

Übung 52: **NAME** / GAME / GALE / SALE / SALT / MALT / MELT / **FELT**

Übung 53: 1. an artist / a painter **2.** an actress / a singer **3.** a philosopher **4.** an astronomer / a mathematician / a physicist **5.** a detective **6.** an actor / a comedian **7.** an author / a writer / a novelist **8.** a conductor **9.** a guitarist **10.** a navigator / an explorer / an adventurer / a discoverer

Übung 54:

1 L	2 O	S	3 T		4 N
5 I	N		6 O	N	E
7 F	L	8 E	W		W
9 E	Y	E		10 A	
		11 L	12 A	T	13 E
14 S	O		15 M	E	T

130

Übung 55: 1. flat, **flatter, flattest** 2. **good**, better, **best** 3. many, **more, most** 4. cool, **cooler, coolest** 5. **bad**, worse, worst 6. thirsty, **thirstier, thirstiest** 7. **narrow**, narrower, narrowest 8. difficult, **more difficult, most difficult** 9. close, **closer, closest** 10. weak, **weaker, weakest**

Übung 56: 1j / 2f / 3h / 4e / 5a / 6g / 7b / 8i / 9c / 10d

Übung 57: 1. lorry, van, car, motorbike, tricycle 2. beach ball, football, golf ball, marble 3. soup ladle, gravy spoon, tablespoon, teaspoon 4. snowman, snowball, ice cube, snowflake 5. melon, mango, apple, plum, cherry 6. sea, lake, pond, puddle, raindrop 7. albatross, eagle, chicken, blackbird, sparrow 8. Canada, the USA, Germany, Great Britain, Holland 9. hippopotamus, lion, wolf, tortoise, mouse 10. battleship, ferry, yacht, rowing boat, canoe

Übung 58: steady **boyfriend** / should have been **engaged** / he asked me to **marry** him / such a lovely **wedding** / all those **divorced** couples / I'd be a **granny/grandma** / middle-aged **housewife** / to provide their **parents** with **grandchildren** / talk with my **eldest** / my future **son-in-law**

Übung 59: 1. next month 2. this year 3. last week 4. last night 5. Tomorrow 6. today 7. next week 8. yesterday 9. tonight 10. yesterday evening; the night before 11. this morning 12. Sunday afternoon

Übung 60: 1. banana 2. snowman 3. spaghetti 4. alarm clock 5. book 6. toothpaste 7. handkerchief/hankie 8. chain 9. frog 10. encyclopaedia 11. silver 12. bus stop

Übung 61: 1. second 2. spring 3. east 4. Wednesday 5. past 6. moon

Übung 62: 1. Greek 2. Russian 3. Egyptian 4. Chinese 5. Japanese 6. American 7. French 8. British/English 9. Italian 10. Dutch

Übung 63: 1. build 2. accept 3. count 4. train 5. tell 6. run 7. collect 8. spend 9. knit 10. mend

Übung 64: go back **to** the job centre / was looking **for** / working **at** London Zoo / applied **for** the job / filled **in** the application form / hear any more **about** it / phone call **from** the family / **on** their short list / come **for** an interview **at** their home **in** South Kensington / arrived **at** their house / in and **out** of various rooms / **in** the hall / **in** their armchairs / **up** and down on the sofas, climbed **onto** tables / swung **from** the curtains / doubts **about** this particular job / on the point **of** saying so / came running up **to** me / affection **for** a stranger / **on** the spot / **on** my way out / got **to** the gate / whispered **in** my ear

Übung 65: 1. stand up / get up 2. mend/fix/repair 3. empty 4. heavy 5. colour 6. sour 7. lose 8. interesting/exciting 9. rich 10. awake

Übung 66: 1. walk 2. sail 3. swim 4. climb 5. travel 6. sing 7. sell 8. buy 9. steal 10. fly

Übung 67: 1. interval 2. lethal 3. prescription 4. room 5. shade 6. revising 7. lend 8. listen to 9. tall 10. boyfriend 11. notice 12. prize 13. taking 14. road; run 15. greatest 16. gets up 17. job 18. suits 19. take 20. tall

Übung 68:

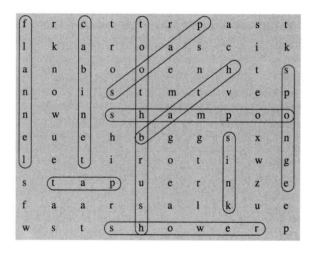

Übung 69: 1. wine 2. medicine 3. clouds 4. flight 5. passport 6. heat 7. orchestra 8. hi-fi 9. theatre 10. goal 11. government 12. prison 13. computer 14. book 15. letter

Übung 70: 1. teeth 2. face 3. neck; shoulders 4. nose; eyes 5. elbows 6. toes 7. backside 8. lips 9. chest 10. feet 11. arms 12. mouth

Übung 71: **RICH** / RICE / NICE / NINE / NONE / GONE / GONG / GANG / BANG / **BANK**

Übung 72:			
playground	chair	magazine	elephant
blackboard	settee	brochure	bear
headmaster	cupboard	comic	crocodile
lesson	table	newspaper	mouse

Übung 73: 1. service 2. possibility 3. silence 4. intelligence 5. definition 6. competition 7. jealousy 8. bravery 9. perfection 10. heat 11. dirt 12. protection 13. hunger 14. preparation 15. dependence 16. weakness 17. pride 18. existence 19. death(s) 20. sadness

Übung 74: 1. take over 2. wallet 3. back 4. sensitive 5. psychological 6. be surprised 7. be afraid/frightened/scared of 8. (cardboard) box 9. mark 10. set meal / set lunch 11. chips 12. department stores 13. take off 14. self-confident 15. imagination 16. get 17. pleasant/likeable 18. studies

Übung 75: 1. roo<u>m in t</u>he 2. <u>love ly</u>chees 3. Fre<u>d ate</u> 4. <u>live ri</u>ght 5. al<u>so apply</u> 6. ha<u>ve to</u> 7. hat<u>e ask</u>ing 8. fa<u>st or e</u>lse 9. Thi<u>s port</u> 10. ho<u>pe ra</u>dical

---

Teil B

Übung 76: 1. Sea 2. Bay 3. Channel 4. River 5. Ocean 6. Lake 7. Falls 8. Delta 9. Gulf 10. Straits

Übung 77: 1. Desert 2. Mountains 3. rainforest 4. steppes 5. Canyon 6. Forest 7. Peninsula 8. Alps 9. Valley 10. Mount

Übung 78:	**AIR**	**WATER**
	glider	ferry
	hot-air balloon	yacht
	jet	speedboat
	supersonic aircraft	submarine
	helicopter	steamer

Übung 79: 1. motorbike 2. double-decker bus 3. truck 4. removal van 5. bicycle 6. tricycle 7. racing car 8. caravan 9. coupé 10. rickshaw

Übung 80: **1.** frost **2.** lightning **3.** thunder **4.** wind **5.** sticky **6.** bright **7.** ice **8.** snow **9.** hailstone **10.** puddle

Übung 81: **1.** police **2.** doctor **3.** interior decorator **4.** gasman **5.** fire brigade **6.** ambulance **7.** electrician **8.** window cleaner

Übung 82: **1.** skyscraper **2.** mosque **3.** terraced house **4.** cottage **5.** igloo **6.** church **7.** mud hut **8.** mansion **9.** synagogue **10.** semi-detached house

Übung 83: 1f / 2h / 3e / 4a / 5j / 6i / 7d / 8g / 9b / 10c

Übung 84: **1.** bank **2.** recycled **3.** catalytic converter **4.** cans **5.** waste **6.** exhaust fumes **7.** greenhouse **8.** rubbish dump **9.** recycling **10.** ozone

Übung 85: **1.** runway **2.** check in **3.** hand luggage **4.** gate **5.** passport control **6.** departure lounge **7.** duty-free (*auch* duty-free shop) **8.** seatbelt **9.** boarding pass **10.** stopover

Übung 86: watching **television** / got the **stereo** on / wants a **CD player** / big new **speaker**s / put a **satellite dish** on the roof / twenty **channel**s / **Walkman** plugged into her ears / wireless or **gramophone** / on the **video**

Übung 87: **1.** unemployed **2.** dole money **3.** apply **4.** curriculum vitae **5.** interview **6.** promotion **7.** pay rise **8.** lunch break **9.** job satisfaction **10.** redundant **11.** self-employed **12.** notice

Übung 88: **1.** traffic **2.** limit **3.** traffic **4.** ...belt **5.** motorway **6.** signs **7.** accidents **8.** ...lights/...lamps **9.** driver **10.** cycle **11.** pedestrian **12.** overtake

Übung 89: **1.** cold **2.** allergic **3.** backache **4.** sore throat **5.** flu **6.** rheumatism **7.** measles **8.** appendicitis **9.** temperature **10.** stomach-ache

Übung 90: **1.** typewriter **2.** ruler **3.** screen **4.** desk **5.** tea break **6.** diary **7.** boss **8.** typing error **9.** staple **10.** envelope

Übung 91: **1. Prime** Minister **2. Chancellor** of the Exchequer **3. Foreign** Secretary **4. Home** Secretary **5. Shadow** Cabinet **6.** House of **Commons** **7. Mr** Speaker **8. Madam** Speaker **9.** Question **Time** **10. Leader** of the Opposition

Übung 92: **1.** exam **2.** school **3.** University **4.** class **5.** teacher **6.** subject **7.** library **8.** course **9.** pupil **10.** homework **11.** exercise **12.** qualification

134

Übung 93: gave me a **cheque** / bank **account** / fifty-pence **coin** / porcelain **piggy bank** / start earning **interest** / the age of the **cash dispenser** / applying for a **credit card** / foreign **currency** / small **change** / I could **spend** money / weekly **pocket money** / paying off my **debts** / the **pound**s will look after themselves

Übung 94: **1.** biscuits – *Kekse* **2.** bill – *Rechnung* **3.** petrol – *Benzin* **4.** underground – *U-Bahn* **5.** ground floor – *Erdgeschoß* / first floor – *erster Stock* **6.** pavement – *Bürgersteig* **7.** timetable – *(hier) Flugplan* **8.** parcel – *Päckchen* **9.** toilets/lavatories – *Toiletten* **10.** tap – *(Wasser)Hahn*

Übung 95: 1h / 2j / 3n / 4p / 5q / 6d / 7l / 8k / 9b / 10f / 11a / 12e / 13r / 14i / 15g / 16c / 17o / 18m

Übung 96: **1.** phonecard **2.** dial **3.** phone box **4.** long-distance **5.** telephone directory **6.** operator **7.** yellow pages **8.** switchboard **9.** answerphone **10.** cordless phone

Übung 97: **1.** press **2.** commercial TV **3.** newspaper **4.** journalist; editor **5.** newsreader **6.** censorship **7.** headline **8.** magazine **9.** circulation **10.** article

Übung 98: **1.** flat; apartment **2.** third floor; fourth floor **3.** sorry!; excuse me! **4.** autumn; fall **5.** letterbox; mailbox **6.** holiday(s); vacation **7.** lift; elevator **8.** torch; flashlight **9.** cinema; movies / movie theater **10.** handbag; purse **11.** trousers; pants **12.** chips; (French) fries **13.** motorway; highway/freeway **14.** shop; store **15.** sweet; candy **16.** jam; jelly **17.** driving licence; driver's license **18.** rubbish; garbage **19.** boot; trunk **20.** (bank)note; bill

Übung 99: keen **photographer** / camera **equipment** / four **lenses** / a **wide-angle** lens / architectural **shots** / a **telephoto** for close-ups / there's my **tripod** / use a **flashlight** / I prefer **slide** film / have **prints** made / a big **screen** / cameras and **accessories**

Übung 100: **1.** trumpet **2.** grand piano **3.** saxophone **4.** cymbals **5.** organ **6.** bass guitar **7.** double bass **8.** bagpipes **9.** accordion **10.** mouth organ **11.** violin **12.** bassoon **13.** drums **14.** castanets **15.** harpsichord

Glossar

Die Zahlen beziehen sich auf die Übungen. Der Einfachheit halber wurde bei Berufs- und Nationalitätsbezeichnungen generell nur die männliche Entsprechung im Deutschen wiedergegeben.

about *über* 64
accept *akzeptieren* 63
accordion *das Akkordeon* 100
account *das Konto* 93
accountant *der Buchhalter* 95
across *über* 12
actor *der Schauspieler* 53, 69
actress *die Schauspielerin* 10, 53
add *addieren* 22
address book *das Adreßbuch* 21
admiral *der Admiral* 35
adult *der Erwachsene* 36
adventurer *der Abenteurer* 53
advice *der Rat(schlag)* 49
aerial *die Antenne* 34
aeroplane *das Flugzeug* 13
afraid: be – of *Angst haben vor* 74
afternoon *der Nachmittag* 36, 59
aircraft *das Flugzeug* 13, 29
airline *die Fluggesellschaft* 15
alarm clock *der Wecker* 60
alcohol-free *alkoholfrei* 56
allergic *allergisch* 89
Alps *die Alpen* 77
a.m. *morgens* 54
ambulance *der Krankenwagen* 81
American *amerikanisch* 62; *der Amerikaner* 14
and *und* 22
answer *die Antwort* 28
answerphone *der Anrufbeantworter* 96
appendicitis *die Blinddarmentzündung* 89
apple *der Apfel* 25
apply for *sich bewerben um* 64, 87
appointment *der Termin* 6
archer *der Bogenschütze* 83
architect *der Architekt* 95
arm *der Arm* 70
armchair *der Sessel* 19
around *um... herum* 26
arrival *die Ankunft* 28
article *der Artikel* 91
artist *der Maler* 13, 53
asleep: be – *schlafen* 32
astronaut *der Astronaut* 95
astronomer *der Astronom* 53
at *an* 26, 64; *in* 64; *auf* 26
ate *Imperfekt von* eat
Austrian *der Österreicher* 14
author *der Autor* 10, 53
avenue *der Boulevard* 31
avocado *die Avocado* 25

awake *wach* 65

baby *das Baby* 36
back *die Rückseite* 74
backache *die Rückenschmerzen* 89
backside *der Hintern* 70
bad *schlecht, schlimm* 55
bagpipes *der Dudelsack* 100
baker's *die Bäckerei* 20
ball game *das Ballspiel* 13
banana *die Banane* 25, 60
bang *der Knall* 71
bank *die Bank* 6, 20, 34, 71
bank note *der Geldschein* 17
bass guitar *die Baßgitarre* 100
bassoon *das Fagott* 100
bat *der Schläger* 23, 83
bath *das Bad* 68
bathroom *das Badezimmer* 18
bay *die Bucht, (hier) der Golf* 76
bear *der Bär* 72
bear *ertragen* 47
beautiful *schön* 2
bed *das Bett* 3, 51
bedroom *das Schlafzimmer* 18
beer *das Bier* 33, 38, 56
beetroot *die rote Beete* 25
begin *anfangen* 4
Belgian *der Belgier* 14
bench *die (Sitz)Bank* 6
bicycle *das Fahrrad* 29, 79
big *groß* 67
biochemist *der Biochemiker* 95
bird *der Vogel* 38
biscuit *der Keks* 44
black *schwarz* 2
blackberry *die Brombeere* 23
blackboard *die Tafel* 72
boarding pass *die Bordkarte* 85
boil *(Wasser, Eier usw.) kochen* 6
boiled potatoes *die Salzkartoffeln* 48
book *das Buch* 40, 60, 69
bookshop *die Buchhandlung* 20
borrow *(sich) leihen* 67
boss *der Chef* 90
bottle bank *der Altglascontainer* 84
bow and arrow *Pfeil und Bogen* 83
bowl *die Schüssel* 42
box *der Kasten* 29; *der Karton* 74
boy *der Junge* 2
boyfriend *der Freund* 41, 67
brake *bremsen* 47

136

Brandenburg Gate *das Brandenburger Tor* 31
bravery *der Mut* 73
bread *das Brot* 8
breakfast *das Frühstück* 3
bridge *die Brücke* 15, 31
briefcase *die Aktentasche* 34
bright *heiter* 80
bring *bringen* 4, 67
British *britisch* 62
brochure *der Prospekt* 72
Buckingham Palace *der Buckingham-Palast* 31
build *bauen* 63
building *das Gebäude* 13
bus stop *die Bushaltestelle* 60
butcher's *die Metzgerei* 20
butter *die Butter* 8, 44
buy *kaufen* 66
by *von* 26
by car *mit dem Auto* 12

cabbage *der Weißkohl* 25
cab driver *der Taxifahrer* 95
cabinet *der (Badezimmer)Schrank* 68
cake *der Kuchen* 11, 48
calculator *der Rechner* 95
camel *das Kamel* 34
camera *die Kamera* 95
can *die Dose* 84
Canadian *der Kanadier* 14
canoeist *der Kanufahrer* 83
canyon *der Cañon* 77
captain *der Kapitän* 35
car *das Auto* 13, 22, 34, 40
caravan *der Wohnwagen* 79
cardboard box *der Karton* 74
card game *das Kartenspiel* 13
care —> take
carpenter *der Tischler* 95
carrot *die Möhre, die Karotte* 25
cash dispenser *der Geldautomat* 93
castanets *die Kastagnetten* 100
castle *das Schloß* 18
catalytic converter *der Katalysator* 84
CD player *der CD-Spieler* 86
cellar *der Keller* 47
censorship *die Zensur* 97
chain *die Kette* 60
chair *der Stuhl* 72
champagne *der Champagner* 33
chancellor *(hier) der Kanzler* 35
change *das Kleingeld* 93
channel *der Fernsehkanal* 86
Channel *der (Ärmel)Kanal* 76
check in *einchecken* 85
check-in desk *der Abfertigungsschalter* 56
cheese *der Käse* 44
chef *der Küchenchef* 10
chemist *die Apotheke* 20
cheque *der Scheck* 17, 93
chest *die Brust* 70
chick *das Küken* 36
chicken *das Huhn* 36

child *das Kind* 36, 41
chimney-sweep *der Kaminkehrer* 95
chin *das Kinn* 16
Chinese *chinesisch* 62
chips *die Pommes frites* 8, 48, 74
chisel *die Meißel* 95
chocolate *die Schokolade* 34, 48
choose *wählen, sich aussuchen* 4
church *die Kirche* 82
cider *der Apfelwein* 33
circulation figures *die Auflage* 97
city *die Großstadt* 36
class *die Unterrichtsstunde* 92
clever *gescheit* 30
climb *klettern, steigen* 66
cloakroom *die Garderobe* 6
close *nahe* 55
clothes *die Kleider* 13
clothing *die Kleidung* 13
cloud *die Wolke* 69
clown *der Clown* 10
club *der (Golf)Schläger* 83
coal *die Kohle* 69
coffee *der Kaffee* 33
coffee-maker *die Kaffeemaschine* 7
coin *die Münze* 17, 93
cold *kalt* 2, 22
cold *die Erkältung* 89
collapse *„zusammenklappen"* 37
collect *sammeln* 63
colour *die Farbe* 13; *Farb...* 65
comedian *der Komiker* 53
comic *das Comic-Heft* 72
commercial TV *das Werbefernsehen* 97
competition *die Konkurrenz* 73
complain *sich beschweren* 5
computer *der Computer* 17, 69
concert *das Konzert* 69
conductor *der Dirigent* 53
contain *enthalten* 32
cook *kochen, zubereiten* 6
cook *der Koch* 95
cooker *der Herd* 7, 42
cool *kühl* 55
cordless phone *das schnurlose Telefon* 96
correct *richtig* 28
cottage *das Cottage, das Häuschen* 82
count *zählen* 63
country *das Land* 13
countryside *die Landschaft* 6
coupé *das Coupé* 79
course *der Kurs* 92
cousin *der Cousin* 24
cream *die Sahne* 48
credit card *die Kreditkarte* 93
cricketer *der Kricketspieler* 83
crime *die Kriminalität* 69
criminal *der Verbrecher* 45
crocodile *das Krokodil* 72
crowded *überfüllt* 40
cruel *grausam* 30
cup *die Tasse* 42
cupboard *der Schrank* 72
curl *sich locken* 22

137

currency *die Währung* 93
curriculum vitae *der Lebenslauf* 87
cutlery *das Besteck* 38
cymbals *die Becken* 100
Cypriot *der Zypriot* 14

dangerous *gefährlich* 2
dark *dunkel* 2
date *die Verabredung* 6, 75
daughter *die Tochter* 24
day *der Tag* 36
death *der Tod* 3, 73
debts *die Schulden* 93
decorator *der Maler* 10
deer *das Reh* 47
definition *die Definition* 73
delta *das Delta* 76
dentist *der Zahnarzt* 95
department store *das Warenhaus* 74
departure gate *der Flugsteig* 85
departure lounge *die Abflughalle* 85
dependence *die Abhängigkeit* 73
desert *die Wüste* 77
desk *der Schreibtisch* 90
detective *der Detektiv* 53
dial *wählen* 96
diary *der Terminkalender* 90
dictionary *das Wörterbuch* 51
difficult *schwierig* 55
dirt *der Schmutz, der Dreck* 73
disc jockey *der Diskjockey* 10
discoverer *der Entdeckungsreisende* 53
disease *die Krankheit* 13, 69
dishwasher *die Spülmaschine* 7
disk *die Diskette* 69
diver *der Taucher* 83
do *machen* 4, 22, 27, 37
do the ironing *bügeln* 5
do sports *Sport treiben* 5
do some work *arbeiten* 5
doctor *der Arzt* 10, 81
dog *der Hund* 13, 38
Doge's Palace, the *der Dogenpalast* 31
dole money *das Arbeitslosengeld* 87
double bass *der Kontrabaß* 100
double-decker bus *der Doppeldecker* 79
down the road *ein Stück weiter die Straße entlang* 12
down: two floors – *zwei Stockwerke tiefer* 2
dozen *das Dutzend* 15
drawing board *das Zeichenbrett* 95
drill *der Bohrer* 95
drink *das Getränk* 51
drop *fallen lassen* 28
drums *das Schlagzeug* 100
Dutch *holländisch* 62
Dutchman *der Holländer* 14
duty-free *der Duty-free-Shop* 85

earth *die Erde* 3
east *der Osten* 61
Easter *Ostern* 15
easy *leicht* 2
eat *essen* 54

editor *der Herausgeber* 97
egg *das Ei* 8, 36, 44, 51
Egyptian *ägyptisch* 62
Egyptian *der Ägypter* 14
eight *acht* 9
elbow *der Ellbogen* 70
electrician *der Elektriker* 81
electricity *der Strom* 15
elephant *der Elefant* 72
eleven *elf* 9
emperor *der Kaiser* 35
empty *leer* 65
encyclopaedia *die Enzyklopädie* 60
English *englisch* 62
Englishman *der Engländer* 41
envelope *der Briefumschlag* 90
evening *der Abend* 36
exam *die Prüfung* 92
exciting *aufregend* 65
exercise *die Übung* 6, 92
exhaust fumes *die Abgase* 84
existence *das Dasein* 73
explorer *der Forscher* 53
eye *das Auge* 54, 70

face *das Gesicht* 16, 70
fall asleep *einschlafen* 28
falls *der (Wasser)Fall* 76
farmer *der Landwirt* 10
fashion model *das Mannequin* 56
fast *schnell* 40
fat *dick* 30
fatal *tödlich* 67
fault *der Fehler, der Defekt* 6
feed *füttern* 37
feel *(sich) fühlen* 4
feet *Plural von* foot
felt *der Filz* 52
ferry *die Fähre* 78
Filipino *der Filipino* 14
fill in *ausfüllen* 64
find *finden* 4
finger *der Finger* 16
fire *das Feuer* 11
fire brigade *die Feuerwehr* 81
fireman *der Feuerwehrmann* 95
first-aid kit *das Verbandszeug* 21
first-class seat *der Sitz erster Klasse* 56
fish *der Fisch* 8, 38, 48
fit *passen* 67
five *fünf* 9, 11
fix *reparieren* 65
flannel *der Waschlappen* 68
flat *die Wohnung* 18
flat *flach* 55
flew *Imperfekt von* fly
flight *der Flug* 69
floor *der Fußboden* 6
floppy disk *die Diskette* 17
flu *die Grippe* 89
fly *fliegen* 4, 54, 66
fly *die Fliege* 23
foot *der Fuß* 16, 41, 70
football *das Fußballspiel* 69

138

footballer *der Fußballspieler* 13, 83
for *für* 64
Forbidden City, the *die Verbotene Stadt* 31
foreign *ausländisch* 6
foreign language *die Fremdsprache* 13
forest *der Wald* 77
forget *vergessen* 4
fork *die Gabel* 3, 42
formula-one driver *der Formel-Eins-
    Fahrer* 83
four *vier* 9
France *Frankreich* 23
freezer *die Gefriertruhe* 7
French *französisch* 62
Frenchman *der Franzose* 14
fridge *der Kühlschrank* 42
fried eggs *die Spiegeleier* 48
friend *der Freund, der Bekannte* 28, 67
frightened: be – of *Angst haben vor* 74
frog *der Frosch* 60
from *von* 64
frost *der Frost* 80
frostbite *die Erfrierungen* 19
fruit *das Obst* 38, 44, 48
frying pan *die Bratpfanne* 7
furniture *die Möbel* 38, 49
furniture shop *das Möbelgeschäft* 20
furry animal *das Pelztier* 40

gale *der Sturm* 52
game *das Spiel* 6, 52
gang *die Bande* 71
garage *die Garage* 20
gardener *der Gärtner* 95
gasman *der Gasmann* 81
generous *großzügig* 30
gentleman *der Herr* 3
gentlemen *Plural von* gentleman
German *der Deutsche* 14, 41
get *bekommen* 74
get lost *sich verlaufen* 5, 53
get rich *reich werden* 5
get up *aufstehen* 65, *(morgens)* 67
get wet *naß werden* 5
gin *der Gin* 8
girl *das Mädchen* 2
glasses *die Brille* 15
glider *das Segelflugzeug* 78
go *gehen* 71; – to school *in die Schule
    gehen* 6
go bad *schlecht werden* 5
go deaf *taub werden* 5
go mad *verrückt werden* 5
goal *das Tor* 69, 83
gold *das Gold* 23
golfer *der Golfspieler* 83
gone *Partizip Perfekt von* go
gong *der Gong* 71
good *gut* 55
government *die Regierung* 69
gramophone *das Grammophon* 86
grandchildren *die Enkelkinder* 24
granddaughter *die Enkelin* 24
grandfather *der Großvater* 24

grandmother *die Großmutter* 24
grand piano *der Flügel* 100
grape *die Traube* 25, 69
grapefruit *die Grapefruit* 25
great *groß(artig)* 67
great-uncle *der Großonkel* 24
greedy *gierig* 30
Greek *der Grieche* 14; *griechisch* 62
green *grün* 17
greenhouse effect *der Treibhauseffekt* 84
grey *grau* 17
ground *der Boden, der Grund* 6
grow *(sich) wachsen lassen* 4
guidebook *der Reiseführer* 21
guitarist *der Gitarrenspieler* 53
gulf *der Golf* 76

hailstone *das Hagelkorn* 80
hair *das Haar, die Haare* 49, 51
hairdresser(`s) *der Friseur* 20, 95
half *die Hälfte* 41
ham *der Schinken* 8
hand *die Hand* 16
handkerchief *das Taschentuch* 60
handkie *das Taschentuch* 60
hand luggage *das Handgepäck* 85
happy *glücklich* 6
hard *hart* 2; *schwierig* 2
hard disk *die Festplatte* 17
hare *der (Feld)Hase* 11, 47
harpsichord *das Cembalo* 100
head *der Kopf* 16
headline *die Schlagzeile* 97
headmaster *der (Schul)Rektor* 72
hear *hören* 67
heart *das Herz* 17
heat *die Hitze* 69, 73
heaven *der Himmel* 3
heavy *schwer* 65
heir *der Erbe* 47
helicopter *der Hubschrauber* 78
helmet *der Helm* 95
help *helfen* 37
hero *der Held* 41
hi-fi *das Hi-Fi* 69
high *hoch* 67
high-heeled boots *Stiefel mit hohen
    Absätzen* 40
hire *mieten* 11
hobby *das Hobby* 41
home *nach Hause* 45
homework *die Hausaufgaben* 92
honest *ehrlich* 30
horse *das Pferd* 83
hot *heiß* 2
hot-air balloon *Heißluftballon* 78
hotel *das Hotel* 51
hour *die Stunde* 36
house *das Haus* 18, 41
Houses of Parliament, the *das Parlaments-
    gebäude* 31
Hungarian *der Ungar* 14
hunger *der Hunger* 73

139

ice *das Eis* 80
igloo *das Iglu* 82
ill *krank* 6
illness *die Krankheit* 13
illustrated *illustriert* 40
imagination *die Phantasie* 74
in *in* 12, 26, 64; *hinein, rein* 54; – the afternoons *nachmittags* 12; – the mornings
morgens 26
indigestion tablets *die Magentabletten* 21
information *die Informationen* 49
intelligence *die Intelligenz* 73
interest *die Zinsen* 93
interesting *interessant* 65
interior decorator *der Maler* 81
interval *die Pause* 67
interview *das Vorstellungsgespräch* 87
into: pay – an account *auf ein Konto
einzahlen* 26
island *die Insel* 15
Italian *der Italiener* 14; *italienisch* 62

Japanese *japanisch* 62
jealousy *die Eifersucht* 73
jet *das Düsenflugzeug* 78
jeweller's *der Juwelier* 20
job *die Stelle* 67
job satisfaction *Befriedigung durch die
Arbeit* 87
journalist *der Journalist* 97

keyboard *die Tastatur* 17
kidney *die Niere* 17
kilo *das Kilo* 41
king *der König* 35
kitchen *die Küche* 18
kiwifruit *die Kiwi(frucht)* 25
knew *Imperfekt von* know
knife *das Messer* 3, 42
knit *stricken* 63
know *wissen* 4, 47

ladder *die Leiter* 95
ladies *Plural von* lady
lady *die Dame* 3, 41
lake *der See* 76
landscape *die Landschaft* 6
language *die Sprache* 13, 32
last *(das) letzte* 6
last night *gestern abend* 45; *heute nacht* 59
last week *letzte Woche* 59
late *spät* 54
lately *neulich* 45
latest *neuest* 6
lay *(hin)legen* 6
lazy *faul* 30
leaf *das Blatt* 41
learn *lernen, sich aneignen* 67
left *links* 2
lend *(aus)leihen* 67
lesson *die Unterrichtsstunde* 72
lethal *tödlich* 67
letter *der Brief* 69; *der Buchstabe* 36
lettuce *der (grüne) Salat* 6, 25, 48

library *die Bibliothek* 20, 34, 92
lie *liegen, sich legen* 6
life *das Leben* 3, 54
light *hell* 2
lightning *der Blitz* 80
likeable *sympathisch* 74
lined *liniiert* 22
lip *die Lippe* 70
listen to *(sich) anhören* 67
literature *die Literatur* 38
liver *die Leber* 17, 75
living room *das Wohnzimmer* 18
long-distance *Fern...* 96
look *gucken* 6
look for *suchen nach* 64
lose *verlieren* 4
lose weight *abnehmen* 65
lovely *(wunder)schön* 75
lucky: be – *Glück haben* 6
lunch *das Mittagessen* 36
lunch break *die Mittagspause* 87
lung *die Lunge* 17

magazine *die Illustrierte* 72, 97
make *machen* 27, 37
make a fuss *Umstände machen* 5
make a noise *Krach machen* 5
male *männlich* 32
malt *das Malz* 52
mandarin *die Mandarine* 25
mansion *die Villa* 82
many *viele* 55
map *die (Land)Karte, der Stadtplan* 15
mark *die Note* 74
market *der Markt* 20
match *das Streichholz* 15
mathematician *der Mathematiker* 53
meal *das Essen, die Mahlzeit* 51
measles *die Masern* 89
medicine *die Medizin* 69
melon *die Melone* 25
melt *schmelzen* 52
mend *reparieren* 63, 65
metropolis *die Metropole* 36
microphone *das Mikrofon* 95
microscope *das Mikroskop* 95
microwave *das Mikrowellengerät* 7
midday *der Mittag* 36
milk *die Milch* 3, 44
mineral water *das Mineralwasser* 48
mint *die Minze* 75
mistake *der Fehler* 6
money *das Geld* 17
monitor *der Computerbildschirm* 17
month *der Monat* 36, 59
moon *der Mond* 61
morning *der Morgen* 36
Moroccan *der Marokkaner* 14
mosque *die Moschee* 82
mother-in-law *die Schwiegermutter* 41
motorbike *das Motorrad* 79
mountains *das Gebirge* 77
Mount Fuji *der Fudschijama* 77
mouse *die Maus* 41, 72

mouth *der Mund* 70
mouth organ *die Mundharmonika* 100
mow *mähen* 37
much *viel* 45
mud hut *die Lehmhütte* 82
museum *das Museum* 23
mushroom *der Pilz* 48
music *die Musik* 38, 51, 69

name *der Name* 52
narrow *eng* 55
nationality *die Nationalität* 69
navigator *der Seefahrer* 53
near *in der Nähe von* 12; *nahe* 22
nearest *nächst(gelegen)* 6
neck *der Hals* 16, 70
needle *die Spritze* 95
nephew *der Neffe* 24
nervous *nervös* 30
new *neu* 54
New Zealander *der Neuseeländer* 14
news *die Nachricht* 49
newsagent's *der Zeitungshändler* 20
newspaper *die Zeitung* 15, 19, 72, 97
newspaper headline *die Schlagzeile* 56
newsreader *der Nachrichtensprecher* 97
next *nächst* 6, 59
nice *schön* 71
niece *die Nichte* 24
night *die Nacht* 36; the – before *am Abend vorher* 59
nine *neun* 9, 71
no *nein* 28, 45
noisy *laut* 2
none *keine* 71
noodles *die Nudeln* 48
nose *die Nase* 70
notice *bemerken* 67
notice: hand in one's – *kündigen* 87
novelist *der Romanschriftsteller* 53
nuisance *die Nervensäge* 45
nurse *die Krankenschwester* 95
nut *die Nuß* 48
nylon stockings *die Nylonstrümpfe* 40

oar *das Ruder* 83
ocean *der Ozean* 76
off-licence *die Wein- und Spirituosenhandlung* 20
on *auf* 26, 64; be – the point of ... *dabei sein, zu* ... 64; – the spot *auf der Stelle* 64; – Sunday *am Sonntag* 12
one *eins* 9
one day *eines Tages* 54
onion *die Zwiebel* 23, 25
only *erst* 54
onto *auf... hinauf* 64
opera *die Oper* 75
operator *die Vermittlung* 96
opposite *gegenüber von* 12
orange *die Apfelsine* 15, 25
orange juice *der Orangensaft* 33
orchestra *das Orchester* 69
organ *die Orgel* 100

out of *aus* 26; *aus ... heraus* 64
oven *der Ofen* 95
over *über* 12
ozone hole *das Ozonloch* 84

page *die Seite* 69
paintbox *der Malkasten* 23
painter *der Maler* 13, 53
pair *das Paar* 47
paper *das Papier* 3
paragraph *der Absatz* 36
parking space *der Parkplatz* 56
pass *bestehen* 67
passport *der Reisepaß* 21, 69
passport control *die Paßkontrolle* 85
past *die Vergangenheit* 61
pasta *die Nudeln, die Teigwaren* 48
patient *geduldig* 30
patrol car *der Streifenwagen* 95
pause *das Zögern, das Schweigen* 67
pay *(be)zahlen* 32
pay rise *die Gehaltserhöhung* 87
pea *die Erbse* 25
pen *der Füller* 32; *(auch) der Kuli* 3
pencil *der Bleistift* 15
peninsula *die Halbinsel* 77
pepper *der Pfeffer* 3
perfection *die Perfektion* 73
philosopher *der Philosoph* 53
phone box *die Telefonzelle* 96
phonecard *die Telefonkarte* 96
photograph *das Foto* 34
photographer *der Fotograf* 95
physicist *der Physiker* 53
piggy bank *das Sparschwein* 93
pilot *der Pilot* 10, 69
pink *rosa* 17
place *die Stelle* 67
plate *der Teller* 42
play *das Theaterstück* 6
playground *der Spielplatz* 72
pleasant *sympathisch* 74
plum *die Pflaume* 25
pocket money *das Taschengeld* 93
police *die Polizei* 81
policeman *der Polizist* 95
polite *höflich* 30
politics *die Politik* 69
pope *der Papst* 35
pop music *die Popmusik* 56
port *der Portwein* 33
possibility *die Möglichkeit* 73
postage *das Porto* 69
postman *der Postbote* 10
pot *der Topf* 42
potato *die Kartoffel* 25, 41
pound *das Pfund* 49, 93
practice *das Üben* 6
precious metal *das Edelmetall* 56
preparation *die Vorbereitung* 73
prescription *das (ärztliche) Rezept* 67
present *das Geschenk* 15
president *der Präsident* 35
press *die Presse* 97

141

price *der Preis* 67
pride *der Stolz* 73
prince *der Prinz* 35
princess *die Prinzessin* 35
prison *das Gefängnis* 69
private *privat* 28
prize *der Preis, der Gewinn* 67
promotion *die Beförderung* 87
protection *der Schutz* 73
psychological *psychisch* 74
puddle *die Pfütze* 80
pull *ziehen* 28
pupil *der Schüler* 92
purple *lila* 17
purse *das Portemonnaie* 17
pyjamas *der Pyjama* 49
pyramid *die Pyramide* 23

qualification *die Qualifikation* 92
queen *die Königin* 35
queue *die (Menschen)Schlange* 47
quiet *ruhig* 2

racing car *der Rennwagen* 79, 83
racket *der Schläger* 83
radio *das Radio* 3
railway *die Bahn* 29
raincoat *der Regenmantel* 19
rainforest *der Regenwald* 77
ran *Imperfekt von* run
realize *(be)merken* 6
recipe *das Kochrezept* 67
recognize *wiedererkennen* 6
recycled paper *das Altpapier* 84
recycling *das Recycling* 84
red rose *die rote Rose* 40
Red Square *der Rote Platz* 31
redundant: be made – *arbeitslos werden* 87
remark *(mündlich) bemerken* 67
remember *sich erinnern* 6
remind *(jemanden) erinnern* 6
removal van *der Möbelwagen* 79
rent *die Miete* 15
repair *reparieren* 65
revise *(durch Wiederholung) lernen* 67
rheumatism *das Rheuma* 89
rice *der Reis* 71
rich *reich* 65, 71
rickshaw *die Rikscha* 79
ride *fahren* 47
right *recht* 2; *richtig* 2
river *der Fluß* 76
road *die Straße* 67
roast beef *das Roastbeef* 8
rode *Imperfekt von* ride
roof *das Dach* 18
room *der (verfügbare) Platz* 67
round *um … herum* 26
rubbish dump *der Müllabladeplatz* 84
ruler *das Lineal* 23, 90
run *laufen* 22, 63
run over *überfahren* 67
runway *die Start- und Landebahn* 85
Russian *russisch* 62

sadness *die Traurigkeit* 73
safe *sicher* 2
sail *segeln* 66
salad *der (gemischte) Salat* 6
sale *der Ausverkauf* 32, 52
salt *das Salz* 3, 48, 52
sandwich *das Sandwich* 41
satellite dish *die Satellitenantenne* 86
saucer *die Untertasse* 42
saw *die Säge* 95
saxophone *das Saxophon* 100
scared: be – of *Angst haben vor* 74
scarlet *scharlach(rot)* 17
school *die Schule* 92
scissors *die Schere* 49, 95
Scot *der Schotte* 14
screen *der Bildschirm* 90
sculptor *der Bildhauer* 95
sea *das Meer* 76
search for *suchen nach* 26
seatbelt *der Sicherheitsgurt* 85
second *zweit* 61
see *sehen* 6
self-confident *selbstbewußt* 74
self-employed person *der Freiberufler* 87
sell *verkaufen* 66
semi-detached house *die Doppelhaus-
  hälfte* 82
send *schicken* 47
sensitive *sensibel* 74
sent *Partizip Perfekt von* send
sentence *der Satz* 36
separated *getrennt* 32
service *die Bedienung* 73
set lunch *das Menü* 74
set meal *das Menü* 74
settee *das Sofa* 72
seven *sieben* 9
shade *der Schatten (als Schutz)* 67
shadow *der (klar umrissene) Schatten* 67
shampoo *das Shampoo* 68
sheep *das Schaf* 41
shop *das Geschäft* 13
shoulder *die Schulter* 16, 70
shout *rufen, schreien* 45
shower *die Dusche* 68
show-jumper *der Springreiter* 83
sick *krank*; be – *sich übergeben* 6
sight *das Augenlicht* 47
sign *unterschreiben* 32
silence *das Schweigen* 73
silver *das Silber* 60
sing *singen* 66
singer *die Sängerin* 53
sink *das Waschbecken* 68
sister *die Schwester* 24
sister-in-law *die Schwägerin* 24
six *sechs* 9
sky *der Himmel* 69
skyscraper *der Wolkenkratzer* 82
smoked salmon *der Räucherlachs* 23
snapshot *der Schnappschuß* 19
snip *schnippeln* 45
snorkel *der Schnorchel* 83

snow *der Schnee* 80
snowman *der Schneemann* 60
so *so* 54
soap *die Seife* 34, 68, 75
soapdish *die Seifenschale* 19
soap powder *das Waschpulver* 44
soccer player *der Fußballspieler* 13
soft *weich* 2
sore throat *die Halsschmerzen* 89
soup *die Suppe* 44
sour *sauer* 3, 65
space suit *der Raumanzug* 95
spade *der Spaten* 95
spaghetti *die Spaghetti* 60
Spaniard *der Spanier* 14
sparkling wine *der Schaumwein, der Sekt* 33
speaker *der Lautsprecher* 86
spectacles *die Brille* 15
speedboat *das Schnellboot* 78
spend *ausgeben* 63, 93; *(ver)brauchen* 63;
    verbringen 4
sponge *der Schwamm* 68
spoon *der Löffel* 42
sport *die Sportart* 13; *der Sport* 75
spot *der Fleck* 32
spring *der Frühling* 61
squash player *der Squashspieler* 83
staircase *die Treppe* 18
stand up *sich erheben* 65, 67
staple *die Heftklammer* 90
stationer's *die Schreibwarenhandlung* 20
steak *das Steak* 51
steal *stehlen* 66
steamer *das Dampfschiff* 78
steering wheel *das Lenkrad* 56
steppes *die Steppen* 77
stereo *die Stereoanlage* 86
sticky *schwül* 80
stomach *der Magen* 17
stomach-ache *die Magenschmerzen* 89
stopover *die Zwischenlandung* 85
store *das Lager* 75
straits *die (Wasser)Straße* 76
strange *merkwürdig* 6
street *die Straße* 31, 40, 67
string *der Bindfaden* 32
studies *das Studium* 74
study *das Arbeitszimmer* 18
subject *das Fach* 92
submarine *das U-Boot* 78
sugar *der Zucker* 3, 48
suit *(jemandem) stehen* 67
Sunday *Sonntag* 59
sunglasses *die Sonnenbrille* 21
suntan lotion *die Sonnencreme* 21
supersonic aircraft *das Überschall-
    flugzeug* 78
surprised: be – *sich wundern* 74
sweet *süß* 3
swim *schwimmen* 66
swimming pool *das Schwimmbad* 83
swimsuit *der Badeanzug* 21
switchboard *die Telefonzentrale* 96
synagogue *die Synagoge* 82

table *der Tisch* 72
tablecloth *die Tischdecke* 19
take *nehmen* 11; *(hin)bringen* 67
take a break *eine Pause machen* 5
take care *aufpassen* 11
take the dog for a walk *mit dem Hund spazie-
    rengehen* 37
take an exam *eine Prüfung machen* 27, 67
take a holiday *Urlaub machen* 5
take some medicine *Medizin einnehmen* 5
take off *starten* 74
take over *übernehmen* 74
take a photo *ein Foto machen* 27
tall *groß, hoch* 67; *hoch(gewachsen)* 67
tap *der Wasserhahn* 68
tasty meal *das schmackhafte Essen* 40
taxi *das Taxi* 95
tea *der Tee* 33, 44, 48, 75
tea break *die Teepause* 90
teacher *der Lehrer* 92
teamwork *die Teamarbeit* 19
teenager *der Teenager* 36
teeth *Plural von* tooth
telephone directory *das Telefonbuch* 96
television *der Fernseher* 29, 86
tell *sagen* 4; *erzählen* 63
temperature *das Fieber* 89
ten *zehn* 9
terraced house *das Reihenhaus* 82
Thai *der Thailänder* 14
thanks *der Dank* 49
theatre *das Theater* 69
thin *dünn* 28
think *denken* 4
thirsty *durstig* 55
this morning *heute morgen* 59
this year *dieses Jahr* 59
three *drei* 9
through *durch* 26
thunder *der Donner* 80
thunderstorm *das Gewitter* 19
Tibetan *der Tibeter* 14
tidy (up) *aufräumen* 37
to *in, nach* 26; *nach, zu* 64
toaster *der Toaster* 7
today *heute* 59
toddler *das Kleinkind* 36
toe *die Zehe* 70
toilet paper *das Toilettenpapier* 44
tomato *die Tomate* 25
tomorrow *morgen* 59
tongue *die Zunge* 15
tonic *das Tonic* 8
tonight *heute abend* 59
tooth *der Zahn* 41, 70
toothbrush *die Zahnbürste* 68
toothpaste *die Zahnpasta* 60
top-floor apartment *die Dachgeschoß-
    wohnung* 56
tow (away) *abschleppen* 54
town *die Stadt* 36
train *der Zug* 51
train *abrichten, trainieren, ausbilden* 63
travel *reisen* 66

143

travel agent's *das Reisebüro* 20
traveller's cheque *der Reisescheck* 21
tree *der Baum* 13, 38
tricycle *das Dreirad* 79
trousers *die Hose* 49
truck *der Lastwagen* 79
trumpet *die Trompete* 100
truth *die Wahrheit* 28
Turk *der Türke* 14
turn down *leiser stellen* 32
TV *der Fernseher* 3
TV announcer *der Fernsehansager* 95
twelve *zwölf* 9
two *zwei* 9
typewriter *die Schreibmaschine* 90
typing error *der Tippfehler* 90

ugly *häßlich* 2
umbrella *der Regenschirm* 23
uncle *der Onkel* 24
under *unter* 26
unemployed *arbeitslos* 87
university *die Universität* 92
up: two floors – *zwei Stockwerke höher* 2
up and down *rauf und runter* 64

valley *das Tal* 77
vegetables *das Gemüse* 48
veto *das Veto* 75
video *das Video* 86
video camera *die Videokamera* 21
village *das Dorf* 36
violin *die Geige* 100
visit *besuchen* 6

waist *die Taille* 16
walk *laufen* 66
Walkman *der Walkman* 86
wall *die Wand* 18
wallet *die Brieftasche* 74
war *der Krieg* 28
wardrobe *der Kleiderschrank* 6

warm welcome *die herzliche Begrüßung* 40
wash *waschen* 37
washing machine *die Waschmaschine* 7
waste *der Abfall* 84
watchstrap *das Uhrarmband* 19
water-polo player *der Wasserballspieler* 83
weak *schwach* 55
weakness *die Schwäche* 73
Wednesday *Mittwoch* 61
week *die Woche* 36, 47, 59
weigh *wiegen* 47
what *was* 45
whether *ob* 47
whisky *der Whisky* 33
white *weiß* 2
White House, the *das Weiße Haus* 31
wide awake *hellwach* 65
wife *die Ehefrau* 41
wind *der Wind* 29, 80
window cleaner *der Fensterputzer* 81
windy weather *das windige Wetter* 40
wine *der Wein* 33, 69
with *mit* 26; fall in love – *sich ver-*
    lieben in 12
without *ohne* 48
woman *die Frau* 41
word *das Wort* 36
word processor *das Textverarbeitungs-*
    system 95
work *die Arbeit* 67
wrist *das Handgelenk* 16
write *schreiben* 37, 47
writer *der Schriftsteller* 53, 95
wrong *falsch* 2

yacht *die Jacht* 78
year *das Jahr* 36
yellow pages *die gelben Seiten* 96
yesterday *gestern* 59
yesterday evening *gestern abend* 59
Yorkshire pudding *der Yorkshire Pudding*
    (Teigbeilage zu Roastbeef) 8